# On the Job English

## ARMED FORCES

*Introduction to General Military English*

CARROT HOUSE

**On the Job English - Armed Forces 1**
© Carrot House

All rights reserved. No part of this publication may be reproduced,
stored in a retrieval system, or transmitted in any form or by any means
without the prior permission in writing of Carrot House.

**Printed :** September 2020

**Author :** Carrot Language Lab

**ISBN :** 978-89-6732-251-9

**Carrot Global Inc.**
9F, 488, Gangnam St. , Gangnam-gu, Seoul, 06120, South Korea

# Curriculum Map

| Course | Level 1 | Level 2 | Level 3 | Level 4 | Level 5 | Level 6 | Level 7 |
|---|---|---|---|---|---|---|---|
| **General Conversation** | Essential English: Begin Again | | | | | | |
| | Pre Get Up to Speed 1~2 | New Get Up to Speed+ 1~2 | | | | | |
| | | | New Get Up to Speed+ 3~4 | | | | |
| | | | | New Get Up to Speed+ 5~6 | | | |
| | | | | | New Get Up to Speed+ 7~8 | | |
| | Daily Focused English 1 | | | | | | |
| | Daily Focused English 2 | | | | | | |
| **Discussion** | | | Active Discussion 1 | | | | |
| | | | | Active Discussion 2 | | | |
| | | | | | Dynamic Discussion | | |
| | | | Chicken Soup Course | | | | |
| | | | | Dynamic Information & Digital Technology | | | |
| **Business Conversation** | Pre Business Basics 1 | | | | | | |
| | | Pre Business Basics 2 | | | | | |
| | | | Business Basics 1 | | | | |
| | | | Business Basics 2 | | | | |
| | | | | Business Practice 1 | | | |
| | | | | | Business Practice 2 | | |
| **Global Biz Workshop** | | | | Effective Business Writing Skills (Workbook) | | | |
| | | | | Effective Presentation Skills (Workbook) | | | |
| | | | | | Effective Negotiation Skills (Workbook) | | |
| | | | | | Cross-Cultural Training 1~2 (Workbook) | | |
| | | | | | Leadership Training Course (Workbook) | | |
| **Business Skills** | | | | Simple & Clear Technical Writing Skills | | | |
| | | | | Effective Business Writing Skills | | | |
| | | | | Effective Meeting Skills | | | |
| | | | | Business Communication (Negotiation) | | | |
| | | | | Effective Presentation Skills | | | |
| | | | | | Marketing 1 | | |
| | | | | | | Marketing 2 | |
| | | | | | | Management | |
| **On the Job English** | | | | Human Resources | | | |
| | | | | Accounting and Finance | | | |
| | | | | Marketing and Sales | | | |
| | | | | Production Management | | | |
| | | | | Automotive | | | |
| | | | | Banking and Commerce | | | |
| | | | | Medical and Medicine | | | |
| | | | | Information Technology | | | |
| | | | | Construction | | | |
| | | | Construction English in Use 1 ~ 4 | | | | |
| | | | Public Service English in Use | | | | |

※ This Curriculum Map illustrates the entire line-up of textbooks at CARROT HOUSE.

# ON THE JOB ENGLISH
# ARMED FORCES

# Introduction

**Welcome to Level 1 of the On the Job English - Armed Forces course.**
**This book is an intermediate level course that introduces the learner to basic military English.**

On the Job English - Armed Forces 1 is designed to accustom learners with military English terminology and phrases that can be used in both professional and casual settings, and familiarize them with a variety of situations and concepts commonly encountered in the armed forces. By the end of the course, learners will be able to understand and express a variety of military concepts in English as well as comprehend written and spoken instructions and orders. Each unit introduces key vocabulary related to the topic and gives learners the opportunity to utilize the new vocabulary and concepts through exercises covering all four key language areas: reading, listening, writing, and speaking. The topics covered in the course range from everyday topics such as talking about your day and health issues, to very specific themes such as weaponry and different types of missions.

This book is ideally used in the classroom as there are several activities that require pair work, but it can also be a good source for self-study if the learner's objective is to obtain a better understanding of basic military concepts using the English language. This book is carefully designed so that the different sections all come together to form one coherent lesson that revolves around a common theme. The reading passages provide insight into general topics related to the military while the listening passages reflect realistic conversations learners are likely to encounter in the field. The grammar lessons go over some of the key grammar used in the passages, while the speaking activities allow the learners to talk and express their opinions about the topic covered in the lesson while utilizing the grammatical rules that were previously covered. By the end of a lesson, learners will not only be more knowledgeable about the central topic, but they will also be able to discuss issues related to the topic using real-life terms and phrases.

Participation is the deciding factor of how much a learner can get out of this course. The book contains many exercises that require learners to work with and discuss with classmates, and these exercises are essential in tying together all the different elements learned throughout the lesson. Therefore, learners are strongly encouraged to actively participate throughout the course.

# Components

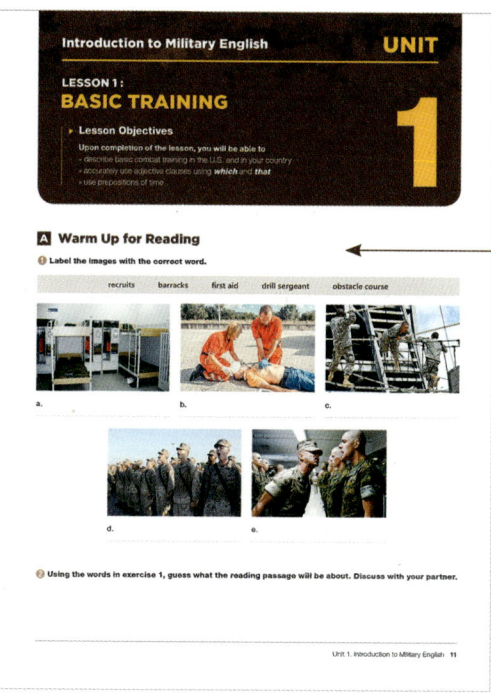

### Warm Up
» Vocabulary exercises to prepare learners for the lesson
» Covers key vocabulary related to reading and listening passages

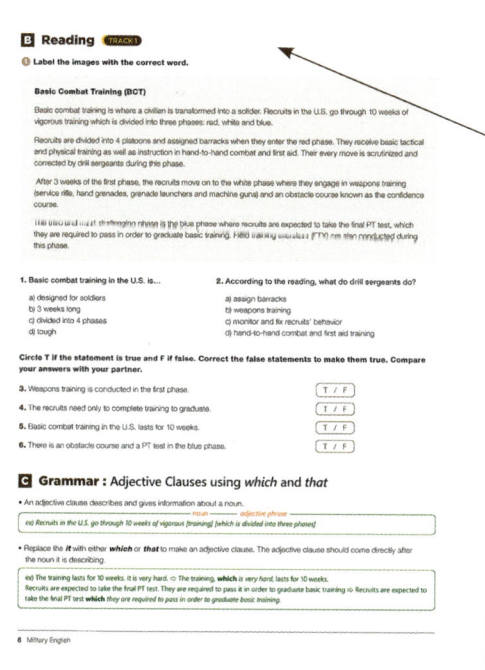

### Reading
» Intermediate-level reading passages containing general information about military topics
» Provides background information essential to the understanding of the listening passage
» Comprehension questions for learners to assess understanding of the passage

# ON THE JOB ENGLISH
# ARMED FORCES

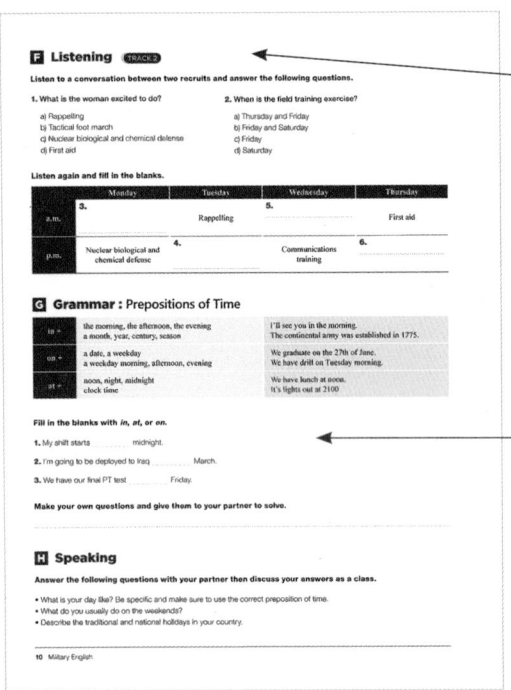

### Listening
» Realistic conversations based on the topic covered in the reading passage
» Comprehension questions for learners to assess understanding of the passage

### Grammar
» Covers key grammar from reading and listening passages
» Comprehension questions for learners to apply grammar in speech

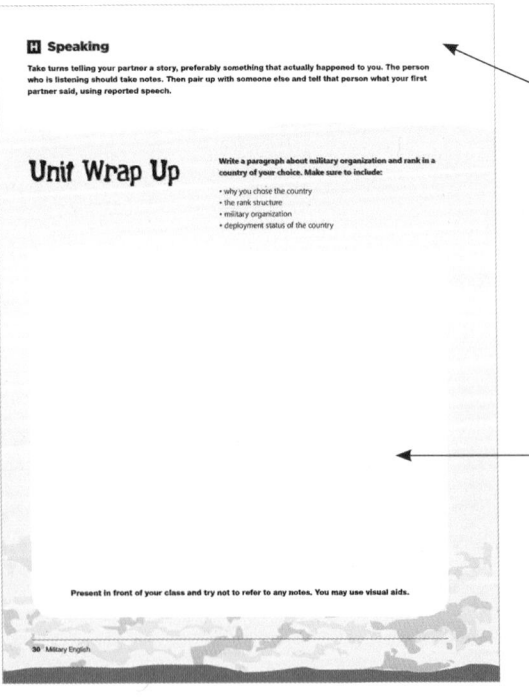

### Speaking
» Discussion questions and role plays to allow learners to express opinions by applying vocabulary, grammar, and knowledge acquired

### Unit Reviews
» Writing and presentation topics related to topic covered in the unit

# Table of Contents

| UNIT | | | | |
|---|---|---|---|---|
| **1** | | **Introduction to Military English** | | |
| | | **Lesson 1**: Basic Training | **Lesson 2**: A Military Life | |
| | Learning Objective | Describe basic combat training in the U.S. | Read and use military time | |
| | Grammar | • Adjective clauses **which** and **that**<br>• Prepositions of time | • Future tense<br>• Past habit | P. 11 / P. 15 |
| **2** | | **Military Structure** | | |
| | | **Lesson 3**: Rank | **Lesson 4**: Military Organization | |
| | Learning Objective | Recognize U.S. military ranks and insignias | Recognize and discuss military organization | |
| | Grammar | • Addressing ranks<br>• Present perfect | • The passive<br>• Reported speech | P. 21 / P. 26 |
| **3** | | **Everyday Life** | | |
| | | **Lesson 5**: On Post | **Lesson 6**: Uniform & Tactical Gear | |
| | Learning Objective | Describe a soldier's life on post | Describe different types of military uniforms and gear | |
| | Grammar | • Conjunctions<br>• **had better** | • Difference between **since** and **for**<br>• Gerunds and infinitives | P. 31 / P. 36 |
| **4** | | **Health** | | |
| | | **Lesson 7**: Exercise & Health | **Lesson 8**: Health & First Aid | |
| | Learning Objective | Describe issues related to army fitness | Discuss first aid in the army | |
| | Grammar | • Frequency expressions<br>• Making comparisons | • Reflexive pronouns<br>• Modal auxiliaries **can** and **may** | P. 41 / P. 46 |
| **5** | | **The Base** | | |
| | | **Lesson 9**: On-base Housing | **Lesson 10**: Getting Around Base | |
| | Learning Objective | Discuss housing options in the military | Read maps | |
| | Grammar | • Phrasal verbs | • Countable and uncountable nouns<br>• Articles | P. 51 / P. 56 |

# ON THE JOB ENGLISH
# ARMED FORCES

# Table of Contents

| UNIT | | | | | |
|---|---|---|---|---|---|
| 6 | **Military Technology** | | | | |
| | | Lesson 11 : History of Military Technology | | Lesson 12 : Modern Military Technology | |
| | Learning Objective | Discuss the history of military technology | P. 63 | Discuss different types of AFVs | P. 68 |
| | Grammar | • Present perfect progressive<br>• Past perfect | | • Superlatives<br>• Preposition combinations | |
| 7 | **Military Exercises** | | | | |
| | | Lesson 13 : War Games | | Lesson 14 : Map Reading | |
| | Learning Objective | Discuss military exercises | P. 73 | Read maps | P. 77 |
| | Grammar | • Repeating comparatives<br>• Double comparatives | | • Accurately give coordinates<br>• Giving location relative to a point of reference | |
| 8 | **Convoys** | | | | |
| | | Lesson 15 : Convoys | | Lesson 16 : Briefings | |
| | Learning Objective | Discuss convoys | P. 83 | Give a briefing | P. 87 |
| | Grammar | • Non-action verbs<br>• Participial adjectives | | • Get + adjective<br>• Get + past participle | |

| Appendix | | |
|---|---|---|
| 1 | LISTENING SCRIPTS | P. 94 |
| 2 | ANSWER KEY | P. 103 |

# UNIT 1-8

On the Job English
**ARMED FORCES**

# Introduction to Military English

## LESSON 1:
## BASIC TRAINING

▶ **Lesson Objectives**

Upon completion of the lesson, you will be able to
» describe basic combat training in the U.S. and in your country
» accurately use adjective clauses using **which** and **that**
» use prepositions of time

**UNIT 1**

## A Warm Up for Reading

**1** Label the images with the correct word.

| recruits | barracks | first aid | drill sergeant | obstacle course |

a. _____

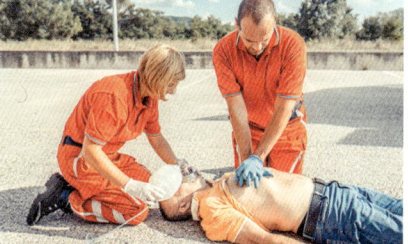

b. _____

c. _____

d. _____

e. _____

**2** Using the words in exercise 1, guess what the reading passage will be about. Discuss with your partner.

## B Reading  TRACK 1

### Basic Combat Training (BCT)

Basic combat training is where a civilian is transformed into a solider. Recruits in the U.S. go through 10 weeks of vigorous training which is divided into three phases: red, white, and blue.

Recruits are divided into 4 platoons and assigned barracks when they enter the red phase. They receive basic tactical and physical training as well as instructions in hand-to-hand combat and first aid. Their every move is scrutinized and corrected by drill sergeants during this phase.

After 3 weeks of the first phase, the recruits move on to the white phase where they engage in weapons training (service rifle, hand grenades, grenade launchers, and machine guns) and an obstacle course known as the confidence course.

The third and most challenging phase is the blue phase where recruits are expected to take the final PT test, which they are required to pass in order to graduate basic training. Field training exercises (FTX) are also conducted during this phase.

1. Basic combat training in the U.S. is…
   a) designed for soldiers
   b) 3 weeks long
   c) divided into 4 phases
   d) tough

2. According to the reading, what do drill sergeants do?
   a) assign barracks
   b) weapons training
   c) monitor and fix recruits' behavior
   d) hand-to-hand combat and first aid training

**Circle T if the statement is true and F if false. Correct the false statements to make them true. Compare your answers with your partner.**

3. Weapons training is conducted in the first phase.   T / F
4. The recruits need only to complete training to graduate.   T / F
5. Basic combat training in the U.S. lasts for 10 weeks.   T / F
6. There is an obstacle course and a PT test in the blue phase.   T / F

## C Grammar : Adjective Clauses using *which* and *that*

An adjective clause describes and gives information about a noun.

ex) Recruits in the U.S. go through 10 weeks of vigorous [training] [which is divided into three phases].
— noun — — adjective phrase —

Replace the **it** with either **which** or **that** to make an adjective clause. The adjective clause should come directly after the noun it is describing.

| | |
|---|---|
| ex) The training lasts for 10 weeks. It is very hard. | ⇨ The training, **which** *is very hard*, lasts for 10 weeks. |
| Recruits are expected to take the final PT test. They are required to pass it in order to graduate basic training. | ⇨ Recruits are expected to take the final PT test **which** *they are required to pass in order to graduate basic training.* |

**Combine the two sentences. Use (b) as your adjective clause.**

**1.** (a) The training transforms civilians into soldiers.     (b) It lasts for 10 weeks.

**2.** (a) The barracks are very clean.     (b) They are assigned at the beginning of training.

**3.** (a) The third phase is the blue phase.     (b) It is the most challenging one.

**Make your own question and give it to your partner to solve.**

## D Speaking

**Answer the following questions with your partner then discuss your answers as a class.**

- What is basic training like in your country? Explain the structure and what kind of training you receive.
- If you have completed basic training, what did you find most difficult? If not, what do you think you will find most difficult? Why?

## E Warm Up for Listening

**Label the images with the correct word.**

| rappelling | map reading | foot march | weapons training |

a.

b.

c.

d.

Unit 1. Introduction to Military English    **13**

## F Listening

**Listen to a conversation between two recruits and answer the following questions.**

1. What is the woman excited to do?
   a) Rappelling
   b) Tactical foot march
   c) Nuclear biological and chemical defense
   d) First aid

2. When is the field training exercise?
   a) Thursday and Friday
   b) Friday and Saturday
   c) Friday
   d) Saturday

**Listen again and fill in the blanks.**

|      | Monday | Tuesday | Wednesday | Thursday |
|------|--------|---------|-----------|----------|
| a.m. | 3.     | Rappelling | 5.     | First aid |
| p.m. | Nuclear biological and chemical defense | 4. | Communications training | 6. |

## G Grammar: Prepositions of Time

| in + | the morning, the afternoon, the evening<br>a month, year, century, season | I'll see you in the morning.<br>The continental army was established in 1775. |
|------|---------------------------------------------------|----------------------------------------------------|
| on + | a date, a weekday<br>a weekday morning, afternoon, evening | We graduate on the 27th of June.<br>We have drill on Tuesday morning. |
| at + | noon, night, midnight<br>clock time | We have lunch at noon.<br>It's lights out at 2100. |

**Fill in the blanks with *in*, *at*, or *on*.**

1. My shift starts _____ midnight.
2. I'm going to be deployed to Iraq _____ March.
3. We have our final PT test _____ Friday.

**Make your own questions and give them to your partner to solve.**

## H Speaking

**Answer the following questions with your partner then discuss your answers as a class.**

- What is your day like? Be specific and make sure to use the correct preposition of time.
- What do you usually do on the weekends?
- Describe the traditional and national holidays in your country.

## LESSON 2: A MILITARY LIFE

**UNIT 1**
Introduction to Military English

▶ **Lesson Objectives**

Upon completion of the lesson, you will be able to
» read and use military time
» accurately use the future tense
» express past habit

### A Warm Up for Reading

**1** Match the times with the way it is read.

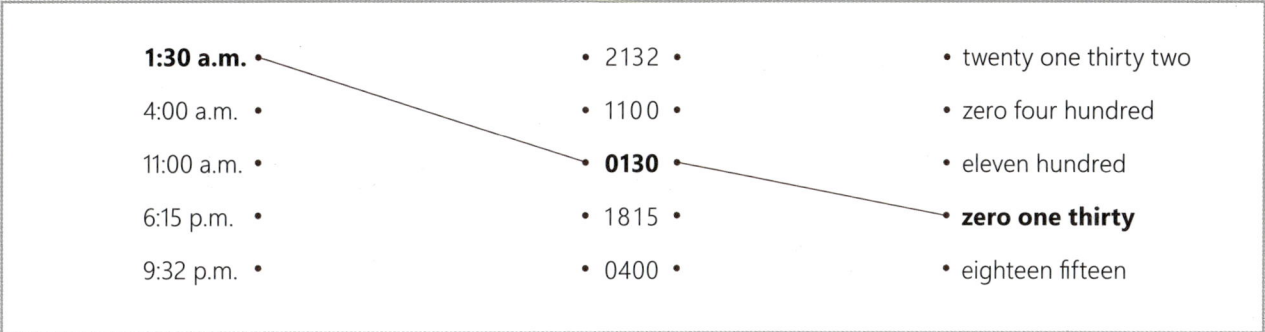

**2** Practice telling military time with a partner.

### B Reading

**Holiday Shopping at the PX**

Get your holiday shopping on at the Post Exchange. Enjoy exclusive discounts on top brands, clothes, jewelry, electronics, furniture, cosmetics, gift cards and more!

Opening hours have been extended for the holiday season for the next two weeks. Operating hours for Sunday through Thursday will be adjusted to 0500 to 2400 from our usual 0500 to 2300 and we will be closing 2 hours later than usual on Fridays and Saturdays at 0300. Please keep in mind that we will be closing early on the 24th at 2100 and be closed for business on the 25th and 26th. You can also enjoy the same discounts and shop a wider variety of goods, 24 hours a day at our online store.

Get more for less and give back to your military family this holiday season by shopping at the Post Exchange!

**1.** The discounts last…

   a) for two weeks
   b) until the holiday season
   c) indefinitely
   d) it's difficult to tell from the passage

**2.** What are the usual closing hours for Saturdays?

   a) 1 a.m.
   b) 1 p.m.
   c) 3 a.m.
   d) 3 p.m.

**3.** What is the purpose of the passage?

**4.** What are the operating hours for the online store?

**5.** How long will the changes to the opening hours last?

**6.** What time will the PX close on the 24th?

## C Grammar : Expressing Future Time

|  |  | be going to | will |
|---|---|---|---|
| **Statement** | I | **am** going to arrive tonight. | **will** arrive tonight |
|  | He / She / It | **is** going to arrive tonight. |  |
|  | You / They / We | **are** going to arrive tonight. |  |
| **Negative** | I | **am not** going to arrive tonight. | **will not (won't)** arrive tonight |
|  | He / She / It | **is not** going to arrive tonight |  |
|  | You / They / We | **are not** going to arrive tonight. |  |
| **Question** | I | **Am I** going to arrive tonight? | **Will** (I) arrive tonight? |
|  | He / She / It | **Is (he)** going to arrive tonight? |  |
|  | You / They / We | **Are (you)** going to arrive tonight? |  |
| **Contraction** |  |  | **I'll / You'll / He'll / She'll / We'll / They'll / It'll** arrive tonight. |

*Use **be going to** or **will** to talk about the future with your partner using the following prompts.*

> *ex) What….. do this weekend?*
> **A:** What are you going to do this weekend?   **B:** I'm going to go out with some friends.

**1.** When… visit your parents?

**2.** What… have for dinner?

**3.** …do anything special for your birthday?

Ask your partner some questions of your own.

## D Speaking

**Answer the following questions with your partner then discuss your answers as a class.**

- Describe what you did yesterday using military time.
- What are you going to do for your next birthday?
- What is the PX like in your country?

## E Warm Up for Listening

**Label the images with the correct word.**

| lights out | PT | personal time | classes |

a.

b.

c.

d.

## F Listening  TRACK 4

**Listen to a conversation between two people and answer the following questions.**

1. When did Sarah enlist in the army?
   a) 2-3 months ago
   b) 2-3 weeks ago
   c) 1 year ago
   d) more than a year ago

2. What did Sarah do to relax?
   a) work out
   b) read a book
   c) sleep
   d) unwind

**Listen again and fill in the blanks.**

| Time | Activity |
|---|---|
| 0430 | 3. |
| 0500 - 0600 | 4. |
| 5. | Breakfast |
| 0900 - 1200 | Classes |
| 6. | Lunch |
| 2100 | 7. |

## G Grammar : Past habit – would / used to / past simple

|  | past habit | past state | happened once |
|---|---|---|---|
| would | We would get an hour for lunch. | X | X |
| used to | We would get an hour for lunch. | I used to be stationed in Greece. | X |
| past simple | We got an hour for lunch. | I was stationed in Greece. | PT was cancelled this morning. |

**Circle the correct phrase(s). Compare your answers with a partner.**

1. I **would be / used to be / was** injured during training.

2. He **would be / used to be / was** my drill sergeant.

3. I **would go / used to go / went** for a run every morning

Look at the conversation script (in the appendix) and identify all the sentences in the past tense. Work with a partner and change the sentences to would be, used to or past simple if possible.

# H Speaking

**1. Tell your partner about your day using the given schedule. Use the past tense and military time. You may add details of your own.**

| Time | Activity |
|---|---|
| 0500 | wake-up |
| 0530-0630 | PT |
| 0700 | breakfast |
| 0830-1200 | class |
| 1200-1300 | lunch |
| 1300-1630 | class |
| 1730 | dinner |
| 1900-2000 | personal time |
| 2100 | lights out |

**2. Create your own weekly schedule. Use military time to present your ideal weekly schedule to the class.**

| Day / Time | Monday | Tuesday | Wednesday | Thursday | Friday | Saturday – Sunday |
|---|---|---|---|---|---|---|
| | | | | | | |
| | | | | | | |
| | | | | | | |
| | | | | | | |
| | | | | | | |
| | | | | | | |
| | | | | | | |

Unit 2. Military Structure

# Unit Wrap Up

**Write a paragraph about basic combat training in a country of your choice. Make sure to include:**

- how long it lasts
- how it is structured
- what kind of classes and training is conducted
- graduation requirements

**Present in front of your class and try not to refer to any notes. You may use visual aids.**

# Military Structure

## LESSON 3:
# RANK

▸ **Lesson Objectives**

Upon completion of the lesson, you will be able to
» recognize U.S. military ranks and insignias
» know how to address people of different ranks
» accurately use the present perfect

**UNIT 2**

## A  Warm Up for Reading

❶ **Match the insignia with the rank.**

| Corporal | First Lieutenant | Sergeant | Colonel | Major General |

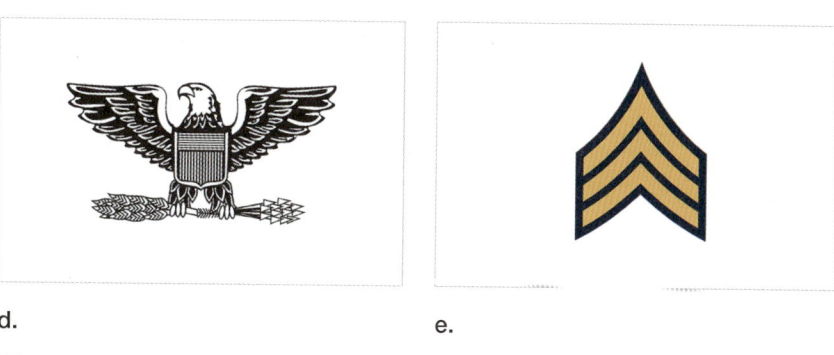

a. _____    b. _____    c. _____

d. _____    e. _____

❷ **What do you know about each of the ranks given in exercise 1? Share your thoughts with a partner.**

## B Reading  (TRACK 5)

**Military Rank Structure**

Military ranks have been around since the Middle Ages and are almost universal in use. They have proven especially advantageous in regards to command and coordination during military operations.

The U.S. military has two main groups: enlisted personnel and commissioned officers. Enlisted personnel make up the majority of the army and are ranked below all commissioned officers. Commissioned officers have received or are receiving training as leaders and have command authority. However, noncommissioned officers (NCO) such as sergeants, and warrant officers, such as technicians and specialists, often have more experience and knowledge than lower ranking commissioned officers. Therefore, it is not uncommon to pair inexperienced junior officers with senior NCO advisors.

**1. Military ranks...**

a) are only used during military operations
b) were used before the Middle Ages
c) are used in almost all countries
d) are used because of tradition

**2. Which one of the following has the highest rank?**

a) NCO
b) Junior commissioned officer
c) Warrant officer
d) Enlisted personnel

Circle T if the statement is true and F if false. Correct the false statements to make them true. Compare your answers with your partner.

**3.** All commissioned officers outrank all enlisted personnel.  T / F

**4.** Rank is determined by experience.  T / F

**5.** You must receive training to become a commissioned officer.  T / F

**6.** The majority of people in the army are NCOs.  T / F

## C Grammar : Present Perfect

The present perfect is used when expressing an event that happened at an unspecified time.

| | | |
|---|---|---|
| **Statement** | Military ranks *have been* around since the Middle Ages. Commissioned officers *have received* training. | **have / has** + past participle |
| **Contraction** | *I've / You've / We've/ They've* received training. *He's / She's* received training | pronoun + **have** = 've  pronoun + **has** = 's |
| **Negative** | He *has not (hasn't) been* promoted yet. I *have not (haven't) seen* the Colonel today. | **have / has** + **not** + past participle |
| **Question** | *Have* you *finished* preparing for the briefing? *Has* Corporal Smith *returned* from the field exercise? Where *have* they *gone*? | **have / has** + subject + past participle |
| **Answer** | Yes, *I have* / No, *I have not* (haven't) Yes, *he has* / No, *he has not* (hasn't) | |

**Work with a partner and practice asking and answering the following questions. Use *ever* in the question.**

> ex) Question: received weapons training
> **Student A:** *Have you ever received weapons training?*
> **Student B:** *Yes, I have / No, I haven't. (Additional information)*

**1.** ride a fighter jet

**2.** win something for free

**3.** traveled with your parents

**4.** be lost

**Make up your own questions and ask your partner.**


## D Speaking

**Answer the following questions with your partner then discuss your answers as a class.**

- What is the military rank system like in your country?
- How is it different from the system in the U.S.?
- What do you think are the advantages and disadvantages of having a rank system?


## E Warm Up for Listening

**Label the images with the correct word.**

| list | altercation | salute | at ease |

a.

b.

c.

d.

Unit 2. Military Structure 23

## F Listening  TRACK 6

**Listen to a conversation between two people and answer the following questions.**

1. Who has the highest rank?

   a) The male speaker
   b) The person who wants the list of new recruits
   c) The female speaker
   d) The person working on the logistics of the field training exercise

2. What problems were there with the new recruits? Choose all that apply.

   a) There was an injury during training
   b) Lack of preparation for the obstacle course
   c) A fight broke out between two of the recruits
   d) Low morale

3. Why did Sergeant Evans go to see the female speaker?

   ......................................................................................................................................

4. What has Corporal Smith been put in charge of?

   ......................................................................................................................................

5. What has Corporal Bennings been put in charge of?

   ......................................................................................................................................

6. What will Sergeant Evans do next?

   ......................................................................................................................................

## G Grammar : Addressing Superiors and Subordinates

|  | Subordinates address | NCOs or officers address |
|---|---|---|
| Pte | X | rank + surname ⇨ Private Moore |
| Cpl and LCpl | Corporal | rank + surname ⇨ Corporal Kim |
| Sgt | Sergeant | rank + surname ⇨ Sergeant Banks |
| SSgt | Staff | Staff |
| WO2 | Sergeant Major | Sergeant Major or Mr./Mrs./Miss + surname ⇨ Mr. Sanchez |
| WO1 | sir (male) or ma'am (female) | Sergeant Major or Mr./Mrs./Miss + surname ⇨ Miss. Smith |
| Commissioned officers | sir (male) or ma'am (female) | X |

**Practice addressing and answering the following with a partner.**

> ex) A: Private Miller          B: Sergeant Jones
>    A: Good morning, Sergeant.  B: Good morning, Private Miller.

**1.** (a) First Lieutenant Ross	(b) Corporal Tanner

**2.** (a) Staff Sergeant Torres	(b) Captain Patterson

**3.** (a) Colonel Ryan	(b) Second Lieutenant Watson

**4.** (a) Specialist Jenkins	(b) Sergeant Major Harris

## H Speaking

**Do the following role plays with a partner. Make sure to address each other appropriately.**

### Role play 1
A: Private Phillips  /  B: Sergeant Manning

Sergeant Manning asks to see Private Phillips about his disruptive behavior. He is having trouble getting along with his fellow soldiers. Talk to Private Phillips to find out what the problem is and help him to resolve it.

### Role play 2
A: Captain Yates  /  B: Corporal Wayne

Corporal Wayne has been put in charge of planning a small get together for the new recruits. Captain Yates asks to see Corporal Wayne to see how the planning is going.

# LESSON 4:
# MILITARY ORGANIZATION

UNIT 2
Military Structure

▶ **Lesson Objectives**

Upon completion of the lesson, you will be able to
» recognize and discuss military organization
» accurately use the passive
» accurately use reported speech

## A  Warm Up for Reading

**Label the symbols with the correct words.**

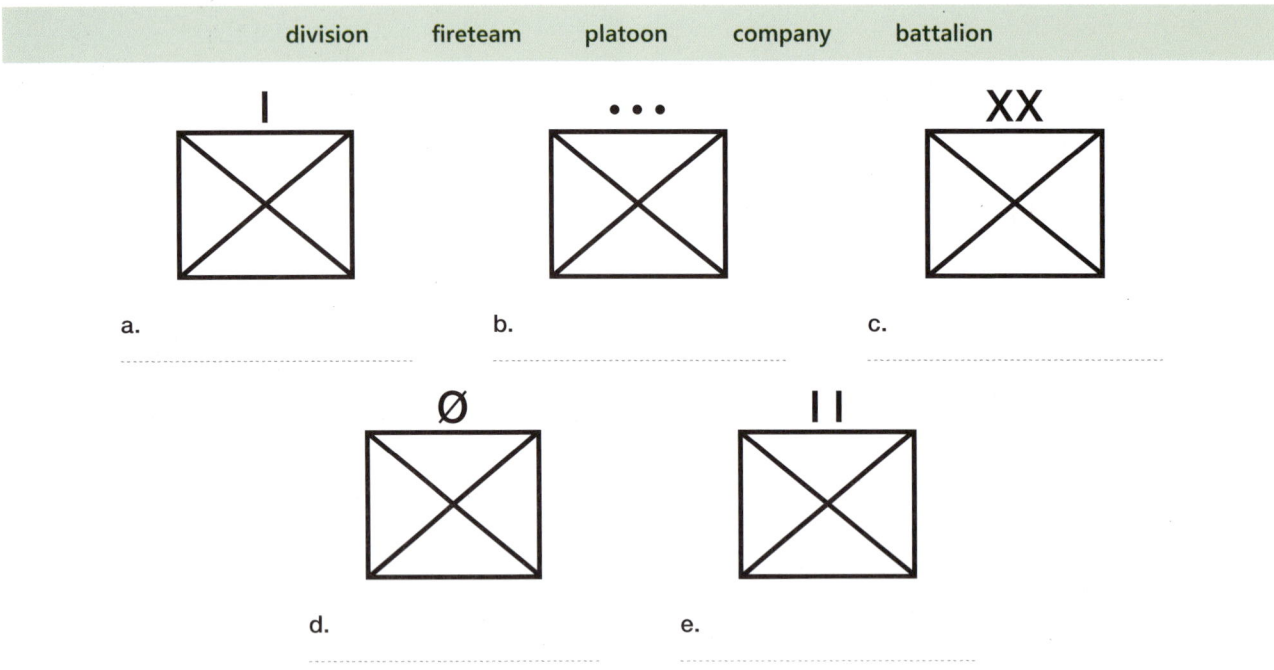

division    fireteam    platoon    company    battalion

a. _____    b. _____    c. _____

d. _____    e. _____

## B  Reading  TRACK 7

**Military Organization**

The use of a hierarchical structure in the military came into widespread use with the Roman army and is still used in modern times due to its effectiveness in managing and commanding the armed forces.

A fireteam, which is made up of four to five soldiers, is the smallest unit in a modern day army and is commanded by a corporal. Two to three fireteams come together to form a squad, and three to four squads form a platoon. The former is commanded by a corporal or sergeant and the latter by a lieutenant. A battalion has anywhere between 300 to 1500 troops, and a division is made up of 10,000 to 20,000 soldiers. An army refers to a unit with more than 100,000 soldiers. Only a general can command units consisting of more than 10,000 troops.

1. Which is not true about military organization according to the passage?

   a) The military is hierarchically organized.
   b) It became popular during the Roman Empire.
   c) The modern day military still uses it.
   d) It helps to manage the commanding ranks.

2. Which is true about a division?

   a) It is made up of 10 battalions.
   b) It has more than 100,000 soldiers.
   c) It is commanded by a general.
   d) A division is the largest unit in the military.

**Fill in the table.**

| Unit | Number of soldiers | Commander |
| --- | --- | --- |
| 3. | 4-5 | Corporal |
| Squad | 8-16 | 4. |
| 5. | 300-1500 | Lt. Colonel |
| Division | 6. | General |

## C  Grammar : The Passive

The subject in an active sentence becomes the object in a passive sentence, and the object in the active sentence becomes the subject in the passive.

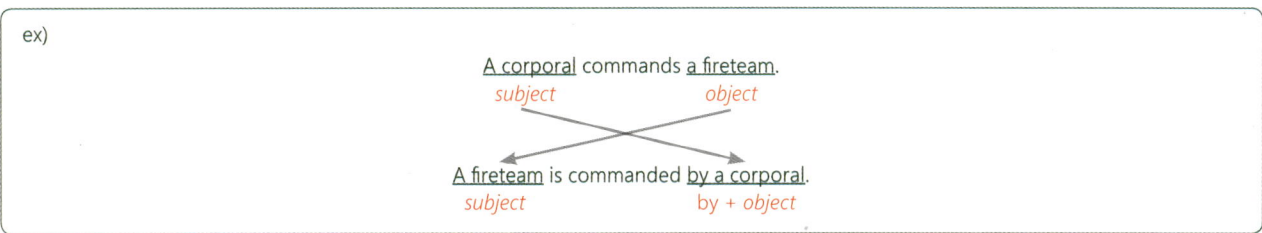

ex)
A corporal commands a fireteam.
   subject              object

A fireteam is commanded by a corporal.
   subject                   by + object

Passive sentences are formed using the **be** verb and the **past participle**.

ex)
A hierarchical military structure **was used** by the Romans.
The latter **is commanded** by a lieutenant.

**Change the following sentences to passive.**

1. The modern day military uses a hierarchical structure because of efficiency.

**2.** A lieutenant commands a platoon.

**3.** The colonel must sign the order.

**Make your own questions and swap with a partner.**

## D Speaking

**Answer the following questions with your partner then discuss your answers as a class.**

- What is the military organization like in your country?
- How is it different from the U.S.?
- What do you think are the advantages and disadvantages of having such a system?

## E Warm Up for Listening

**Fill in the blank with the correct word.**

| command | checkpoint | patrol | squad |
| --- | --- | --- | --- |

**1.** Corporal, if the Sergeant becomes indisposed, you are next in _____.

**2.** A Corporal or a Sergeant typically commands a _____.

**3.** I've received a report that there's been extra activity in the city. I want your platoon to _____ the area.

**4.** We set up a _____ at the base of the hill.

## F Listening (TRACK 8)

**Listen to a conversation between two people and answer the following questions.**

**1.** What kind of mission is second platoon being sent on?

   a) Recon
   b) Reserve
   c) Patrol
   d) Evacuation

**2.** Who will be responsible for setting up the checkpoints?

   a) Corporal Robinson
   b) Sergeant Oaks
   c) Corporal Wrenn
   d) Corporal Stone

28  On the Job English _ Armed Forces 1

**Fill in the blanks.**

**3.** First squad is led by _____ .

**4.** Third squad will be _____ for this mission.

**5.** The checkpoint will be situated at _____ .

**6.** What is Lieutenant Hart likely to do next?

_____

## G  Grammar : Reported Speech

Reported speech is used when we report something that someone said to another person. The verb forms in reported speech is as follows.

| Quoted Speech | Reported Speech |
| --- | --- |
| He said "I **train** 5 days a week." | He said he **trained** 5 days a week. |
| He said "I **am training** 5 days a week." | He said he **was training** 5 days a week. |
| He said "I **trained** 5 days a week." | He said he **had trained** 5 days a week. |
| He said "I **am going** to train 5 days a week." | He said he **was going to train** 5 days a week. |
| He said "I **will train** 5 days a week." | He said he **would train** 5 days a week. |
| He said "I **can train** 5 days a week." | He said he **would train** 5 days a week. |

**Change the quoted speech to reported speech.**

**1.** Captain Lone said, "I want to see Lieutenant Hart as soon as possible."

_____

**2.** Lieutenant Hart said, "Corporal Stone is going to be in command of second squad."

_____

**3.** Sergeant Oaks said, "I commanded second squad in Alpha company."

_____

**Make your own questions and swap with a partner.**

_____

# H Speaking

Take turns telling your partner a story, preferably something that actually happened to you. The person who is listening should take notes. Then pair up with someone else and tell that person what your first partner said, using reported speech.

# Unit Wrap Up

Write a paragraph about military organization and rank in a country of your choice. Make sure to include:

- why you chose the country
- the rank structure
- military organization
- deployment status of the country

Present in front of your class and try not to refer to any notes. You may use visual aids.

# Everyday Life

## LESSON 5:
## ON POST

### UNIT 3

▶ **Lesson Objectives**

Upon completion of the lesson, you will be able to
» describe a soldier's life on post
» connect ideas using conjunctions
» use the expression **had better**

## A Warm Up for Reading

**1** Label the images with the correct word.

| command center | dining hall | post office | billets |

a. ..................

b. ..................

c. ..................

d. ..................

**2** Using the words in exercise 1, guess what the reading passage will be about. Discuss with your partner.

## B Reading (TRACK 9)

### A Soldier's Life

A post is where a soldier spends most of his time. It is a military site that houses equipment and provides shelter for personnel in the form of barracks, billets, or quarters. It can also be used as grounds for training and act as a command center. It is oftentimes referred to as a fort or garrison.

Most posts have basic facilities such as a post office and a post exchange (PX), but many would agree that the most important would be the dining facilities (DFACs). The meals provided in the dining hall are called A-Rations or garrison rations and consist of fresh or frozen foods that must be cooked. Individual MRE (Meal, Ready to Eat) are handed out on the field and First Strike Rations (FSR), which have double the calories of MRE, are used when soldiers are on the move.

**1.** Which is not a function of a post?

a) provides entertainment options for the troops
b) stores equipment
c) provides housing for assigned personnel
d) provides meals

**2.** When are First Strike Rations distributed?

a) when there aren't any dining facilities
b) while on a 3 day march
c) when in the field
d) during a field training exercise

Circle T if the statement is true and F if false. Correct the false statements to make them true. Compare your answers with your partner.

**3.** A billet allows soldiers to purchase equipment.  T / F

**4.** One MRE feeds only one person.  T / F

**5.** Garrison rations don't necessarily have to be cooked.  T / F

**6.** All posts have a PX.  T / F

## C Grammar : Connecting Ideas

| | | |
|---|---|---|
| and | adding information | A post is a military site that houses equipment *and* provides shelter for personnel. |
| or | giving alternatives | A-Rations consist of fresh *or* frozen foods |
| but | unexpected, different, or contradictory information | There are many facilities, *but* the most important is the DFAC. |
| so | cause and effect | The field exercise will last two days, *so* we'll be taking the First Strike Rations. |

Fill in the blanks with *and*, *or*, *but*, or *so*.

**1.** The PX was closed _____ I couldn't get any detergent.

**2.** Should we take the MRE _____ FSR?

**3.** Our post has a DFAC _____ it doesn't have a post office.

**4.** I'm going to need to see Sergeant Ross _____ Corporal Lewis.

**Make your own question and give it to your partner to solve.**

## D Speaking

**Answer the following questions with your partner then discuss your answers as a class.**

- What aspect of being a soldier do you think you will find the most difficult?
- How is it different from the U.S.?
- What are the military posts like in your country?

## E Warm Up for Listening

**Label the images with the correct word.**

| MRE | A-ration | case | First Strike Rations |

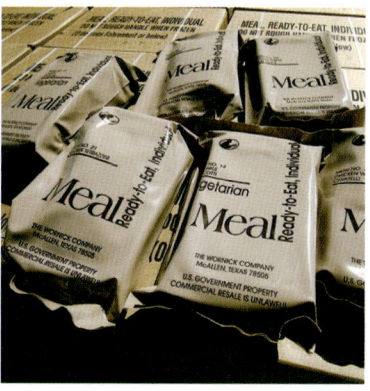

a.

b.

c.

d.

## F Listening  TRACK 10

**Listen to a conversation between two people and answer the following questions.**

1. What are they waiting for?

   a) MREs
   b) Personnel
   c) A-rations
   d) First Strike Rations

2. Why is there a delay in getting resupplied?

   a) There aren't many MREs left.
   b) Lack of personnel.
   c) The mission is lasting too long.
   d) They still have First Strike Rations.

3. How many MREs do they have left?

   .................................................................................................................................................

4. How long will they have to wait until they are resupplied?

   .................................................................................................................................................

5. What type of rations will they have to rely on?

   .................................................................................................................................................

6. Who gave them the news about the delay?

   .................................................................................................................................................


## G Grammar : Had Better

**Had better** is a form of expressing advice and has the same basic meaning as **should** and **ought to**.

| | |
|---|---|
| statement | We **had better** make them last. |
| negative | We **had better** not waste any of the supplies. |
| contraction | I**'d better** speak to the platoon Sergeant again. |

**Take turns giving advice based on the following prompts. State possible consequences if applicable.**

> ex) I'm failing at PT.
> **Speaker A:** I'm failing at PT.
> **Speaker B:** You'd better start working out or you're going to fail the final PT test.

1. I'm always broke at the end of the month.

   .................................................................................................................................................

**2.** I'm feeling under the weather today. I think I'm coming down with something.

**3.** I haven't booked my tickets home yet.

**4.** There are only 2 seats left on the tour to the beach this weekend.

# H Speaking

**Answer the following questions with your partner then discuss your answers as a class.**

- What are the military posts like in your country?
- What kind of facilities do they have and what are they like?
- What do you think life on post would be like?

# LESSON 6 :
# UNIFORM & TACTICAL GEAR

**UNIT 3**
Everyday Life

▶ **Lesson Objectives**

Upon completion of the lesson, you will be able to
» describe different types of military uniforms and gear
» differentiate between *since* and *for*
» accurately use gerunds and infinitives

## A  Warm Up for Reading

❶ Label the images with the correct word.

| ASU | ACU | camouflage | rucksack | flask |

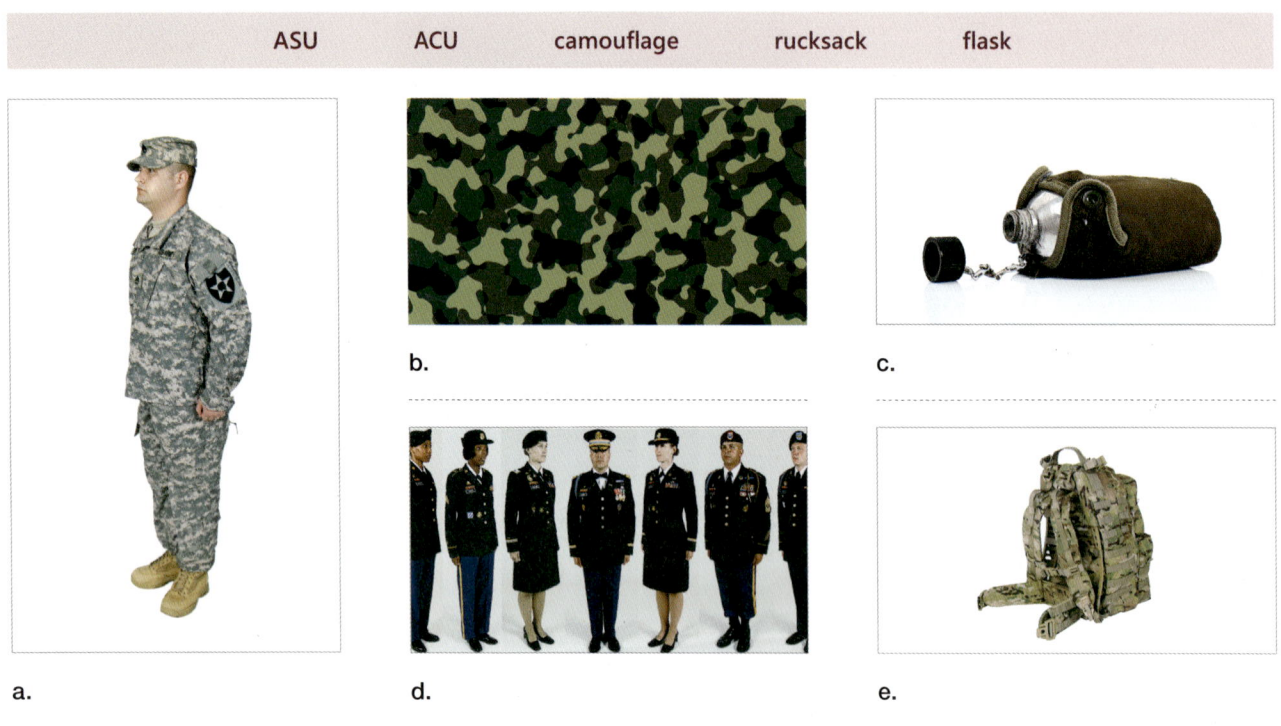

a.

b.

c.

d.

e.

❷ Using the words in exercise 1, guess what the reading passage will be about. Discuss with your partner.

## B Reading  TRACK 11

**Military Uniform**

There are two types of uniforms in the U.S. army. The Army Service Uniform (ASU) is considered formal dress and can be worn to most public and official functions. The Army Combat Uniform (ACU) is used in combat situations.

The current ACUs have been in use since 2004 and use the Universal Camouflage Pattern (UCP) which is effective in multiple environments including desert, forest and the city. A basic field uniform is made up of a jacket, trousers, headgear, t-shirt, and footwear. The Modular Lightweight Load-carrying Equipment (MOLLE) system has been in use since 1997 to carry equipment in the field. It is comprised of a vest (TAP), rucksack, hydration bladder, and modular pouches. A webbing system called Pouch Attachment Ladder System (PALS) allows the extra pouches and smaller equipment to be attached to the vests and backpacks.

**1.** In which situation would an ASU be worn?
 a) army ball
 b) during PT
 c) on patrol
 d) on post

**2.** What is the purpose of the PALS?
 a) It helps web the uniform.
 b) It provides additional camouflage.
 c) It allows the user to attach additional items to the MOLLE.
 d) It makes it easier to carry all the gear.

**Fill in the blanks with words from the reading passage.**

**3.** When attending functions such as weddings and ceremonies, one is expected to wear _____.

**4.** _____ vary slightly from country to country but almost all of them have some sort of camouflage.

**5.** A _____ is a receptacle that stores small quantities.

**6.** _____ is the preferred method of carrying equipment in a number of NATO armed forces, including the U.S.

## C Grammar : Since and For

**Since** and **for** is used to express the duration of an action.

| | | |
|---|---|---|
| since | - is followed by a specific point in time<br>- means that the action began in the past and continues to the present | ACUs have been used *since* 2004. |
| | - the present perfect tense is used with *since* | The MOLLE system has been in use *since* 1997. (O)<br>The MOLLE system is being used *since* 1997. (X) |
| | - a time clause (subject + verb) may also follow *since* | The MOLLE system became popular *since* 9/11 happened. |
| for | - is followed by length of time | The same gear has been used *for* the last 20 years. |
| | - use of present perfect = action continues to present<br>- use of simple past = action ended in past | I've had this uniform *for* 10 years.<br>(I still have the uniform.)<br>I had the uniform *for* 10 years.<br>(I don't have the uniform anymore.) |

**Use *since* or *for* to describe yourself using the following prompts.**

> ex) smoke
> → I've smoked since I was 16. *or*   → I've smoked for 10 years. *or*   → I've never smoked.

1. be in the military
2. study English
3. want to be a soldier
4. have a driver's license

## D Speaking

**Answer the following questions with your partner then discuss your answers as a class.**

- What is the military uniform like in your country?
- How do you think military uniform could be improved?
- What is the purpose of uniforms? How do they affect the wearer?

## E Warm Up for Listening

**Label the images with the correct word.**

| frame | shoulder straps | hydration sack | communication gear |

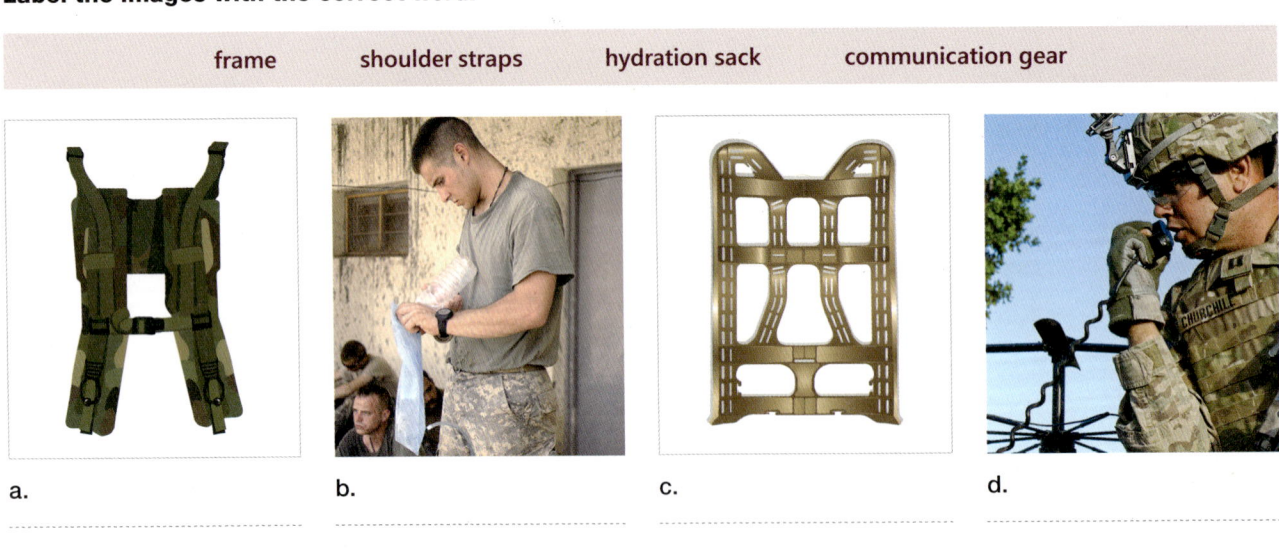

a.   b.   c.   d.

## F Listening (TRACK 12)

**Listen to a conversation between two people and answer the following questions.**

1. What is happening in this conversation?

   a) The woman is showing the man what he should pack in his field gear.
   b) The man and the woman are taking a class on field gear.
   c) The woman is teaching the man how to assemble a MOLLE pack.
   d) The woman is showing the man the components of a MOLLE pack.

**2. Why should the rucksack be assembled horizontally?**

a) Because you could get injured while assembling the rucksack.
b) Because the rucksack will be too heavy.
c) Because you want to make sure the balance is right.
d) Because there are too many items to pack.

**Circle T if the statement is true and F if false. Correct the false statements to make them true. Compare your answers with your partner.**

**3.** A MOLLE pack must be assembled before use.  T / F

**4.** Larger items should be packed first.  T / F

**5.** Full combat gear weighs approximately 15kg.  T / F

**6.** Ammo should be kept in a secure location in the backpack.  T / F

## G Grammar : Gerunds and Infinitives

Some verbs are followed by a gerund (-ing) and some by infinitives. There are a select few that are followed by both.

| | Common verbs followed by… | |
|---|---|---|
| **gerunds** | consider, discuss, enjoy, finish, keep (on), mind, postpone, put off, quit, stop, think about | You might want to consider packing that first. (O) You might want to consider to pack that first. (X) |
| **infinitives** | agree, appear, decide, expect, forget, hope, intend, learn, mean, need, offer, pretend, promise, refuse, try, want, would like | We decided to stick to the original route. (O) We decided sticking to the original route. (X) |
| **gerunds or infinitives** | begin, can't stand, continue, hate, like, love, start | I can't stand packing my MOLLE. It's such a hassle. (O) I can't stand to pack my MOLLE. It's such a hassle. (X) |

**Create sentences using the given words.**

*ex) continue / walk*
→ I'm going to continue walking 3 times a week to keep in shape.

**1.** enjoy / watching

**2.** seem / be

**3.** finish / work

**4.** refuse / help

**5.** need / see

## H Speaking

**Answer the following questions with your partner then discuss your answers as a class.**

- What kind of things do you pack when going on a trip?
- What are some useful items to take on a trip that you would like to recommend to your partner?
- What things do you think you'd need to pack when packing for combat and why?

# Unit Wrap Up

**Write a paragraph about military uniform in a country of your choice. Make sure to include:**

- why you chose the country
- the types of uniforms
- interesting features

**Present in front of your class and try not to refer to any notes. You may use visual aids.**

# Health

## LESSON 7:
## EXERCISE & HEALTH

### ▶ Lesson Objectives

**Upon completion of the lesson, you will be able to**
» describe issues related to army fitness
» accurately use frequency expressions
» make comparisons

UNIT  4

## A  Warm Up for Reading

**1** Label the images with the correct word.

| push-ups | sit-ups | pull-ups | 2 mile run | swimming |

a.

b.

c.

d.

e.

**2** Using the words in exercise 1, guess what the reading passage will be about. Discuss with your partner.

Unit 4. Health  41

## B Reading

**Army Fitness**

Physical training is an integral part of military life and soldiers are expected to maintain a certain level of physical fitness while serving in the army. They run every morning and go to the gym two to three times a week. Many soldiers swim once a week or participate in other forms of physical activity such as football, martial arts, or tennis.

Active soldiers are required to take the Army Physical Fitness Test (APFT) at least twice a year. The test measures physical strength and endurance through three events: push-ups, sit-ups and a two mile run. Soldiers are given 2 minutes to do as many push-ups and sit-ups as they can, and their 2 mile run is timed. They must receive a minimum of at least 60 out of 100 points for each event to pass, and whether or not they pass will determine their eligibility for promotions, transfers, and army schools.

**1.** What event is not included in the APFT?

a) pull-ups
b) push-ups
c) sit-ups
d) 2 mile run

**2.** According to the passage, which of the following are examples of physical activities soldiers do to keep fit?

a) weightlifting
b) skiing
c) jiu-jitsu
d) baseball

Circle T if the statement is true and F if false. Correct the false statements to make them true. Compare your answers with your partner.

**3.** A score of 180 is considered a pass on the APFT.  T / F

**4.** Soldiers must take the APFT once a year.  T / F

**5.** Soldiers must pass the APFT to be considered for promotions.  T / F

**6.** Swimming is mandatory to keep in shape in the army.  T / F

## C Grammar : Frequency Expressions (How often)

**How often** asks about frequency.

> ex) How often do you run? / I run every morning.

**How many times** is another way of asking how often.

> ex) How many times a year do you have to take the APFT? / At least twice.

The following are frequency expressions you can use to answer **how often** and **how many times** questions.

| | | |
|---|---|---|
| a lot | every | |
| occasionally | every other | |
| once in a while | once a | day/week/month/year |
| not very often | twice a | |
| hardly ever | three times a | |
| almost never | | |
| never | | |

**Work with a partner and take turns asking and answering *how often / how many times* questions using the following prompts.**

ex) work out ⇨ How often do you work out? / I go to the gym 5 times a week and swim on the weekends.

**1.** cook for yourself

**2.** meet up with friends

**3.** be late for class

**4.** read a book

**Make your own question and give it to your partner to solve.**

## D Speaking

**Answer the following questions with your partner then discuss your answers as a class.**

- What do you do to keep in shape and how often do you do it? Why?
- Why do you think being in shape is considered so important?
- Are there any physical fitness tests in your country's military? What is it like? Do you think it is an effective measure of physical fitness?

## E  Warm Up for Listening

**Label the images with the correct word.**

| cargo net | ditch | fence | low wall | wire |

a.

b.

c.

d.

e.

## F  Listening  (TRACK 14)

**Listen to a conversation between two people and answer the following questions.**

1. What is the man's main complaint?

   a) He didn't do well on the PFT last week.
   b) He is having trouble doing push-ups.
   c) He thinks the woman doesn't understand him.
   d) He is worried he won't do well on the obstacle course.

2. How does the woman feel about the man's complaint?

   a) She thinks he should start going to the gym.
   b) She thinks he should try harder.
   c) She thinks he should get in shape.
   d) She thinks he should stop complaining.

3. Which PFT event was the man relatively good at?

4. Why does the man think the woman like the obstacle course?

5. Which obstacles does the man say involve climbing over something?

6. Which obstacle is the man's least favorite?

44  On the Job English _ Armed Forces 1

## G  Grammar : Comparisons

The comparative is used to compare two or more items. It is followed by **than**.

> *ex) I think my core is much **stronger than** my upper body.*

**Make a comparative sentence using the following prompts.**

> *ex) skateboarding / driving  ⇨  Skateboarding is **more exciting than** driving.*

**1.** army / navy

**2.** running / swimming

***as....as*** can be used to compare two items that are equal.

> *ex) The cargo net is **as difficult as** the low wall.*
> *The obstacle course is almost **as tough as** the PFT.*
> *Jumping the fence is not nearly **as bad as** the cargo net.*

**Work with a partner. Take turns completing the sentences using *as...as*.**

> *ex) Medic! We need a medic....  ⇨  as quickly as possible!*

**3.** You are severely out of shape. You should be working out…

**4.** I can't go any faster! I'm going…

## H  Speaking

**Design your own assault course. Switch designs with your partner and explain how to cross the obstacles.**

# LESSON 8:
# HEALTH & FIRST AID

UNIT 4
Health

▶ **Lesson Objectives**

Upon completion of the lesson, you will be able to
» talk about first aid in the army
» accurately use reflexive pronouns
» accurately use modal auxiliaries *can* and *may*

## A  Warm Up for Reading

**1** Label the images with the correct word.

| first aid kit | tourniquet | bandage | gauze | surgical gloves |

a.

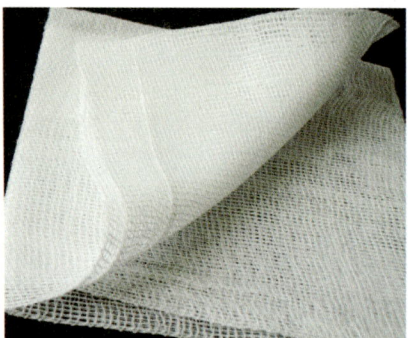
b.

c.

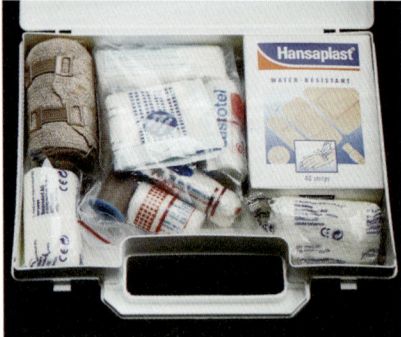
d.

e.

**2** Using the words in exercise 1, guess what you think the reading passage will be about. Discuss with your partner.

## B Reading

**First Aid**

Medics are military personnel who have basic EMT training and are responsible for first aid and trauma care on the battlefield until the injured can receive further help. However, a soldier can bleed out in a matter of minutes depending on the injury and 90 percent of soldiers injured in combat die before they can reach a medical facility. This led to the development of the Army's Improved First Aid Kit (IFAK).

The IFAK is a streamlined version of the full kit that medics carry and weighs less than 500g. It often allows the injured soldiers to apply it themselves and features a one-handed tourniquet (enabling self-application), elastic emergency trauma bandages, hemostatic combat gauze, a nasopharyngeal airway tube, adhesive tape, and surgical gloves. This is especially effective considering the three major causes of death on the battlefield are blood loss, collapsed lungs, and obstructed airways.

**1. Which is true according to the passage?**

a) Medics are trained personnel responsible for treating an array of illnesses.
b) 90 percent of battlefield casualties end up in death.
c) The IFAK was developed due to popular demand.
d) The IFAK is similar to what the medics carry into the field.

**2. Which of the following is a major cause of battlefield fatality?**

a) hemorrhaging
b) infection
c) hyperventilation
d) heart failure

**Circle T if the statement is true and F if false. Correct the false statements to make them true. Compare your answers with your partner.**

3. Medics receive formal training.  T / F
4. Most casualties die before being transported to a medical facility.  T / F
5. An injured soldier can perform first aid on himself using the IFAK.  T / F
6. One of the major causes of death on the battlefield is choking.  T / F

## C Grammar : Reflexive Pronouns

Reflexive pronouns are used when the subject and the object are the same person. They end in **-self** or **-selves**.

> ex) He bandaged **himself**. / I bandaged **myself**. / You bandaged **yourself**.
> They taught **themselves** first aid basics. / We taught **ourselves** first aid basics.

**By** + reflexive pronoun = alone

> ex) Martin went to the gym **by himself**.

**Complete the following the sentences with reflexive pronouns.**

**1.** Don't blame _____. You did everything you could.

**2.** He should stop feeling sorry for _____. He needs to suck it up and make an effort.

**Create sentences with the following prompts. You can use imaginary situations.**

**3.** be proud of yourselves _____

**4.** take care of himself _____

**5.** stop myself _____

## D Speaking

**Answer the following questions with your partner then discuss your answers as a class.**

- Have you ever received first aid training? When? How was it?
- Where can you receive first aid training in your country?
- What would you do if you found an unconscious person?

## E Warm Up for Listening

**Label the images with the correct word.**

| infection | CPR | field dressing | pass out |

a.

b.

c.

d.

## F Listening

**Listen to a conversation between two people and answer the following questions.**

**1. According to the passage, what is the definition of first aid?**

    a) To stop bleeding and prevent infections
    b) To make sure the casualty is breathing
    c) To provide care before the casualty can be seen by a doctor
    d) To keep the casualty alive

**2. What are the three things you must do when you encounter a casualty?**

    a) airway, breathing, circulation
    b) tilt head, lift chin, CPR
    c) restore breathing, stop bleeding, prevent infections
    d) restore breathing, stop bleeding, prevent shock

**3. When should CPR be used?**

**4. What should be used to stop bleeding?**

**5. Name 3 symptoms of shock.**

**6. What does PELCRN stand for?**

## G Grammar : Modal Auxiliaries *can* and *may*

Modal auxiliaries are helping verbs that have a wide range of meanings.

| | | |
|---|---|---|
| **express ability** | can / can't / could / couldn't | *Can* you apply pressure to the wound?<br>I *can't* move my leg. |
| **express possibility** | may / may not / might / might not could | You *may* be able to save your friend's life.<br>It *might* not work.<br>Be careful! He *could* go into shock! |
| **express permission** | may / may not / can / cannot | Sir, *may* I have a word?<br>You *cannot* move the casualties under any circumstances, is that understood? |

**Fill in the blanks with *can, may, might,* or *could*. Use the negative where appropriate. Identify the meaning of the modal.**

**1.** He _____ be going into shock, but we don't have any equipment so there's not much we _____ do.

2. He _____ hold on much longer. How quickly _____ we get a chopper here?

3. This area is off limits. You _____ enter.

4. It's not as simple as we thought. This _____ take a while.

## H Speaking

**Take turns doing the following role play with a partner.**

- You find a wounded soldier on the field. Talk to the soldier to see what is wrong and proceed with first aid. Talk to the casualty through the process to prevent shock.

# Unit Wrap Up

**Create a diet and workout plan and present it in front of the class. Include:**

- the purpose (lose weight, gain muscle, increase stamina etc.)
- a diet and workout plan
- why it is effective
- how soon you would see results

**Present in front of your class and try not to refer to any notes. You may use visual aids.**

# The Base

## LESSON 9 :
## ON-BASE HOUSING

**UNIT 5**

▶ **Lesson Objectives**

Upon completion of the lesson, you will be able to
» talk about housing options in the military
» accurately use phrasal verbs

## A  Warm Up for Reading

① Look at the pictures below and discuss the difference between the two types of housing with a partner. How are they different? What type of people would live in each type of house? How would their lifestyles differ?

② Fill in the blanks with the appropriate word.

| service member | on-base housing | allowance | paycheck | utilities |

a) A/An _____ is compensation an employee receives for his or her work.

b) I have hardly enough to pay for rent yet alone _____ .

c) _____ is limited so we may have to look for housing outside of the military installation.

d) The military gives a/an _____ for people living off base to cover their housing costs.

e) A/An _____ refers to someone who is currently a member of the armed forces.

Unit 5. The Base   51

## B Reading

### On-Base Housing

Free or basically free military housing is generally provided for all service members and can be divided into on-base and off-base housing. On-base housing is provided to all single service members. Soldiers of higher rank can choose to live off base but lower ranking soldiers are required to live on base in barracks or dormitories.

Married service members can choose to live either on or off base, depending on their needs. Soldiers who choose to live off base with their family receive a Basic Allowance for Housing (BAH) with their paycheck to cover housing costs. The amount of the allowance depends on rank, number of dependents, and location. Those that choose to live on base can enjoy free housing and utilities but may have to wait up to a year since most military installations have limited on-base housing. The quality of the house may also vary greatly.

1. Which of the following is true about on-base housing?

   a) All service members are provided with practically free military housing.
   b) Soldiers may choose to live on-base or off-base.
   c) A BAH is provided to all soldiers who choose to live off-base.
   d) Barracks are an example of on-base housing.

2. Choose two things that are considered when deciding the BAH amount.

   a) marital status
   b) number of people in the family
   c) income
   d) where the house is situated

Circle T if the statement is true and F if false. Correct the false statements to make them true. Compare your answers with your partner.

3. Married soldiers can choose to live off base regardless of rank.  T / F
4. Housing, water, and electricity is free for on-base housing.  T / F
5. Married soldiers are guaranteed on-base housing if they wish to live on post.  T / F
6. The houses on base are of excellent quality.  T / F

# C Grammar : Phrasal Verbs

Phrasal verbs are phrases that consist of typically a verb and an adverb or preposition and have a specific meaning.

*ex) depend + on = to rely on*

Phrasal verbs are either separable or non-separable.

| Separable | |
|---|---|
| verb + particle + noun / object | Let's **hand in** the paperwork for the housing. |
| verb + noun / object + particle | Let's **hand** the paperwork **in** for the housing. |
| verb + pronoun + particle | Let's **hand** it **in**. |
| **Non-separable** | |
| verb + particle + noun / pronoun | The BAH amount **depends on** a number of things (O)<br>They **depend on** him (O)<br>They **depend** him **on** (X) |

**The following is a list of common phrasal verbs. Work in groups and complete the table.**

| Phrasal Verb | Type | Meaning | Example |
|---|---|---|---|
| break down | I | | |
| depend on | N | | |
| call off | S | | |
| find out about | N | | |
| get along with | N | | |
| get over | N | | |
| give up | I | | |
| go over to | N | | |

\* **I** = intransitive  **S** = separable  **N** = non-separable

## D Speaking

**Answer the following questions with your partner then discuss your answers as a class.**

- Would you live on base or off-base? Why?
- What do you think are the advantages and disadvantages of living on base?
- What is the military housing situation like in your country?

## E Warm Up for Listening

**Fill in the blanks with the appropriate word.**

| relocate | DoDEA schools | paperwork | throw out | think over |
|---|---|---|---|---|

1. Schools run by the Department of Defense are called _____.
2. I'm going to have to stay at work a little late tonight. I have so much _____ to take care of.
3. These sheets are really old. I think it's about time we _____ them _____.
4. This is a really big decision. I'm going to need some time to _____ it _____.
5. I'm being stationed abroad. My family is going to have to _____ with me.

## F Listening  TRACK 18

**Listen to a conversation between two people and answer the following questions.**

1. What did they decide to do about housing?

   a) The man will go but the woman and the children will stay.
   b) The whole family will relocate to on-base housing.
   c) The whole family will relocate to off-base housing.
   d) The man will go and the woman will stay but she will move out of their current home.

2. Why is the man concerned about relocating?

   a) Because of the language barrier
   b) Because he doesn't believe the schools will be good
   c) Because they are going to have another baby
   d) Because they have too many things

3. Where is the man going to be stationed and when?

   _____

4. Why does the woman want to live on-base?

   _____

5. Why is the man in a rush to submit the paperwork?

   _____

6. How will they get rid of some of their belongings?

## G Grammar: Phrasal Verbs

Here are some more common phrasal verbs. Work in groups and complete the table.

| Phrasal Verb | Type | Meaning | Example |
|---|---|---|---|
| help out | S | | |
| point out | S | | |
| put off | S | | |
| run into | N | | |
| watch out for | N | | |
| write down | S | | |
| clean up | S | | |
| drop in on | N | | |
| figure out | S | | |

\* I = intransitive   S = separable   N = non-separable

## H Speaking

Answer the following questions with your partner then discuss your answers as a class.

- How many times have you moved in your life? How was the experience?
- What was your favorite house?
- Draw your dream house and explain it to your partner.

# LESSON 10:
# GETTING AROUND BASE

**UNIT 5**
The Base

> **Lesson Objectives**
>
> Upon completion of the lesson, you will be able to
> » accurately read maps
> » differentiate between countable and uncountable nouns
> » accurately use articles

## A   Warm Up for Reading

**Look at the map and fill in the spaces with the appropriate phrase.**

| opposite | next to | between | on the corner of | on the right |

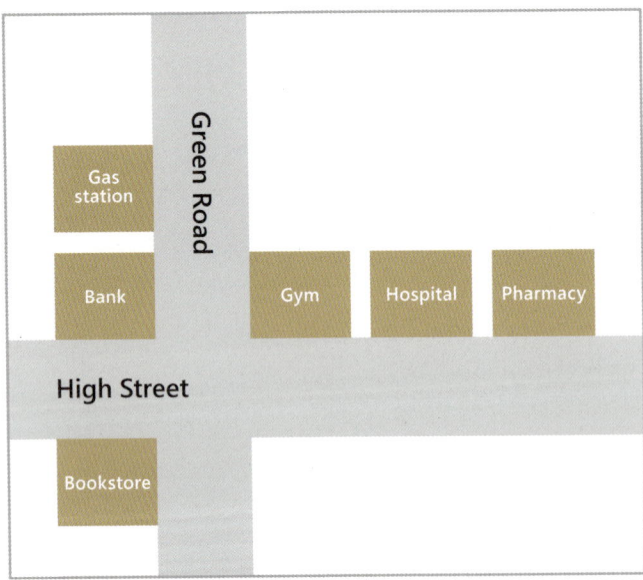

1. The bank is _____ High Street and Green Road.

2. The gas station is _____ the bank.

3. The gym is _____ the bank.

4. The hospital is _____ the gym and the pharmacy.

5. If you walk down Green Road from the gas station in the direction of the bank, you'll see the bookstore _____, by the intersection.

## B Reading

**Read the description below and find the letter that corresponds to each location in the box.**

| Anthony's Pizza ____ | Chapel ____ | Fitness Center ____ | Pharmacy ____ | Post Office ____ | PX ____ |
| Cinema ____ | Grand Hotel ____ | Dental Clinic ____ | Bowling Alley ____ | | |

1. The Fitness Center is on Black Hawk Street next to the shooting range.
2. The dental clinic is on the corner of Lincoln Street and Lee Road.
3. The cinema is on the corner of Lincoln Street and Marion Street, next to the bookstore.
4. The Grand Hotel is on Marion Street. There is a bank next to it.
5. Anthony's Pizza is across the street from the bank.
6. The chapel is on Marion Street before the Family Readiness Center.
7. The PX is opposite the bookstore.
8. The pharmacy is between the PX and dental clinic.
9. Walk towards Lee Road from the pharmacy and make a left. Keep walking until you reach the intersection. The post office will be on your left next to a cafe.
10. The bowling alley is across the road from the post office.

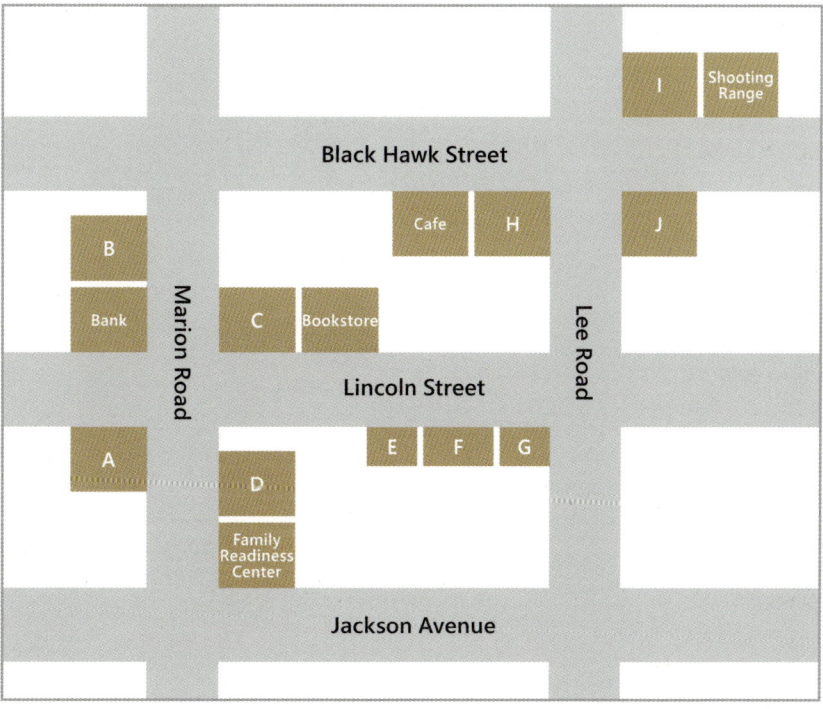

Unit 5. The Base 57

## C Grammar: Countable and Uncountable Nouns

A **countable noun** can be counted, has a plural form, and can be preceded by **a/an** in the singular.

ex) a cookie, one cookie, two cookies…

An **uncountable noun** cannot be counted, does not have a plural form, and cannot be immediately preceded by **a/an**.

ex) a bread (X) one bread (X) two breads (X)

| | Uncountable Nouns |
|---|---|
| whole groups made up of | fruit (apples, bananas, oranges…) <br> sand, flour, rice, salt (made up of tiny granules) |
| individual parts | work (a compilation of things that must get done) |
| liquids | coffee, milk, water |
| solids | bread, meat, butter, gold, paper |
| gases | air, smog, smoke, pollution |
| nature | weather, rain, snow, sunshine |
| abstractions | beauty, fun, happiness, luck, time |

**1. Circle the countable nouns.**

mistake / mail / grammar / pencil / doughnut / sugar / information / diamond / toothpaste / chair / furniture / cup / cheese / letter / chocolate / patience / patient / river / lake

**Add -s or -es if possible and circle the correct verb form.**

**2.** We get a lot of **storm** _____ here in the summer

**3. Gold** _____ (is / are) more expensive than **silver** _____ .

**4.** Do you need any **help** _____ ?

**5.** There (is / are) a lot of **food** _____ in the **refrigerator** _____ .

# D Speaking

**Take turns describing the following maps with your partner. Student should cover the map that is given and draw the map that student A is describing the space provided and vise versa. Check to see how accurately you were able to draw the map!**

### Map A
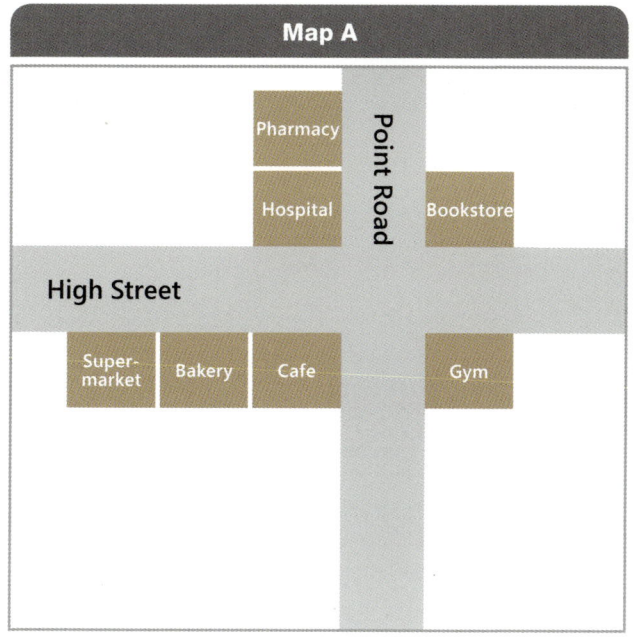

### Draw Map A

### Map B
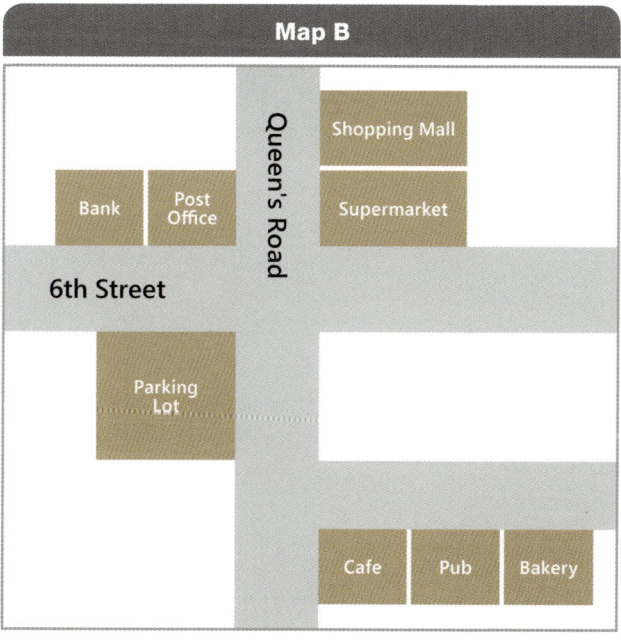

### Draw Map B
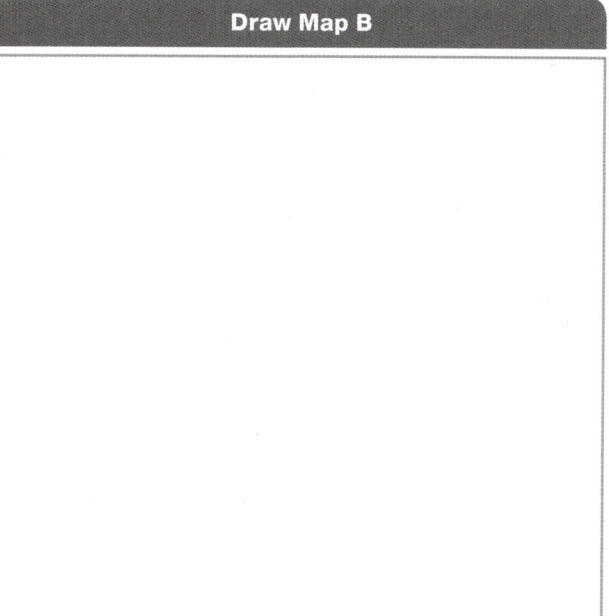

Unit 5. The Base   59

## E Warm Up for Listening

**Fill in the blanks with the appropriate word.**

| sick and tired | go out | sale | hit |

1. I have a couple of hours to burn. I'm going to _____ the gym.
2. I can't stand him anymore! I'm _____ of his complaining!
3. You should get them when they're on _____. You could save a lot of money.
4. I'm go busy. I never get to _____ with my friends anymore.

## F Listening  TRACK 19

**Listen to a conversation between two people and answer the following questions.**

1. Where will the man and woman go? Choose all that apply
   a) Indian restaurant
   b) Greek restaurant
   c) Pub
   d) Shoes R Us

2. Which is true about the Greek restaurant?
   a) It is opposite the post office.
   b) It used to be where the pub was.
   c) The woman has been there before.
   d) It is charging soldiers less.

**Mark the following places on the map.**

| Indian restaurant | Greek restaurant | Pub | Shoes R Us | Pharmacy |

3. _____
4. _____
5. _____
6. _____
7. _____

## G Grammar : Articles

| Nouns | A / an | | The | |
|---|---|---|---|---|
| Singular Countable | Use **a/an** to make a generalization or when talking about one non-specific thing | *A* bank is where you can deposit and withdraw money. I just saw *a* helicopter fly by. | Use **the** in front of singular count, plural countable and uncountable nouns when talking about specific things that both the speaker and the listener know about | I'm going to *the* bank. (both know which bank) *The* helicopter was heading for the city. |
| Plural Countable | X (no article = generalization) | Flowers make me sneeze. | | I love *the* flowers you gave me. |
| Uncountable | X (no article = generalization) | I don't like coffee. | | *The* coffee in *the* dining room is the worst I've ever had. |

**Fill the blanks with *a/an*, *X*, or *the*.**

**A :** What are you planning on doing on the weekend?

**B :** I need to catch up on my reading. I haven't read **1.** _____ book in ages!

**A :** I was going to go to **2.** _____ library this weekend anyway. Want to join me?

**B :** Yeah! That sounds great! How many **3.** _____ books can you check out at a time?

**A :** I think it's five. Want to go for **4.** _____ movie afterwards?

**B :** Sorry, but I don't really like **5.** _____ movies. How about we go for **6.** _____ dinner instead?

**A :** Great!

## H Speaking

**Answer the following questions with your partner then discuss your answers as a class.**

- What kind of facilities did/does your base have? If you have never been on a military base, what kind of facilities would you expect there to be?
- Describe your favorite city or neighborhood in detail. Why do you like it so much?

# Unit Wrap Up

Write a detailed paragraph about your base or your neighborhood. Read your description to your partner. Your partner should try to draw a map based on your description. Check to see how accurate the drawing is.

**Present in front of your class and try not to refer to any notes. You may use visual aids.**

# Military Technology

## UNIT 6

### LESSON 11:
### HISTORY OF MILITARY TECHNOLOGY

▶ **Lesson Objectives**

Upon completion of the lesson, you will be able to
» discuss the history of military technology
» accurately use the present perfect progressive
» accurately use the past perfect

## A  Warm Up for Reading

**1** Label the images with the correct word.

> partisan    cannon    machine gun    helicopter    atomic bomb

a.

b.

c.

d.

e.

**2** Using the words in exercise 1, guess what the reading passage will be about. Discuss with your partner.

## B Reading  TRACK 20

### The History of Weapons

Mankind has been using and developing weapons for warfare, hunting, sport, and self-defense since the prehistoric era, but as is the case with most things, the most marked innovations have taken place since the 20th century.

While medieval weapons such as the halberd, mace, and partisan were still being used during the Renaissance, China had already discovered black powder in the 9th century which led to the invention of the cannon in the 12th century and the firearm in the 13th. The first portable machine gun was invented in 1883 by Hiram Maxim and was used by British troops for the first time in 1893. The 20th century brought about the prototype of the helicopter in 1907 and the use of the first tank in 1916. The world's first atomic bomb, arguably the most destructive weapon in the history of mankind, exploded on the 16th of July, 1945.

**1.** Which of the following is not true according to the passage?

a) Primitive man used weapons.
b) Weapons developed the most in the 20th century.
c) Black powder was invented before the Renaissance.
d) The discovery of black powder enabled the invention of the cannon and the firearm.

**2.** When was the first tank used in battle?

a) During WWI
b) The 19th century
c) 1907
d) Mid 1900s

**Circle T if the statement is true and F if false. Correct the false statements to make them true. Compare your answers with your partner.**

**3.** The machine gun was used in battle in 1893.   T / F

**4.** The helicopter was conceived in 1907.   T / F

**5.** It can be said that the nuclear bomb is the most deadly weapon in the history of mankind.   T / F

**6.** Weapons have gone through major innovation since the 20th century.   T / F

## C Grammar : Present Perfect Progressive

The present perfect progressive expresses how long a present activity has been in progress.

> ex) Mankind **has been using** weapons <u>since the prehistoric era</u>.

It takes the form of **have/has + been + -ing** for statements and **have/has + subject + been + -ing** for questions.

> ex) Weapons **have been evolving** at an astounding rate <u>since the 20th century</u>.
> How long **have humans been using** weapons for?

**Complete the sentences using either the present progressive or the present perfect progressive.**

1. The main assault rifle we (use) _____ right now is the M4. We (use) _____ this model since 1994.

2. We (drive) _____ tanks towards the site as we speak. We (try) _____ to penetrate the enemy site for weeks.

3. We (work on) _____ this project for 2 months. I need a change in scenery.

**Take turns answering the following questions with your partner. Provide as much detail as you can.**

4. How long have you been studying English?

5. How long have you been in the army? How long have you been interested in joining the army?

## D Speaking

**Answer the following questions with your partner then discuss your answers as a class.**

- What do you know about the history of weapons? Share what you know with your partner.
- Why do you think it took so long for firearms to reach the Western world?
- Have you ever used any weapons? Describe your experience.

## E Warm Up for Listening

**Label the images with the correct word.**

tank    battering ram    trebuchet    mortar

a. _____    b. _____    c. _____    d. _____

Unit 6. Military Technology   65

# F Listening  TRACK 21

**Listen to a conversation between two people and answer the following questions.**

**1.** What is true about AFVs?

    a) It is a mobile vehicle that provides protection while possessing offensive capabilities.
    b) It is one of the most effective and destructive weapons we have today.
    c) It is the predecessor to the modern tank.
    d) It was conceived in 1485.

**2.** Put the following in chronological order and write the date if applicable.

    _____ a) Improvements are made to the design.

    _____ b) They are used in battle.

    _____ c) The initial design was developed.

    _____ d) Design for the prototype of the first tank is adopted.

**Fill in the blanks with words from the passage.**

**3.** The idea of AFVs _____ that of the internal combustion engine.

**4.** _____ such as battering rams and trebuchets are the earliest examples of AFVs.

**5.** The woman thinks battering rams and trebuchets are too _____ to be considered AFVs.

**6.** The Renault FT light tank's standout features include the _____ turret and the engine in the back.

# G Grammar : Past Perfect

The past perfect is used when talking about two separate events that happened in the past at different times. It is formed by combining **had** with the **past participle**.

> ex) The first tank **had** already **been used** in battle by the time the Renault FT light tank was developed.
> People **had conceptualized** AFVs before the invention of the internal combustion engine.

**Read the following and identify the order of events. Put 1 next to the event that happened first and 2 next to the event that happened later.**

**1.** The troops pulled out. They had won the battle.

    _____ a) The troops pulled out.

    _____ b) They won the battle.

**2.** Tanks were not used until WWI. They had not been invented yet.

    _____ a) Tanks weren't used until WWI.

    _____ b) Tanks weren't invented yet.

**Make 3 sentences using the past perfect tense.**

1. _____
2. _____
3. _____

## H Speaking

**Answer the following questions with your partner then discuss your answers as a class.**

- What do you know about the history of AFVs? Share what you know with your partner.
- Have you ever been in or seen an AFV? If not, do you know any stories related to AFVs? Share with your partner.
- What do you think were some historical events that drove innovation in military technology?

# LESSON 12:
# MODERN MILITARY TECHNOLOGY

UNIT 6

Military Technology

▶ **Lesson Objectives**

Upon completion of the lesson, you will be able to
» discuss different types of AFVs
» accurately use superlatives
» accurately use different preposition combinations

## A  Warm Up for Reading

**1** Label the images with the correct word.

| amphibious vehicle | artillery | troop carrier | air defense vehicle |

a. ......................  b. ......................  c. ......................  d. ......................

**2** Do you have any experience with any of the items in exercise 1? Share with your partner and your class.

## B  Reading  TRACK 22

**Types of AFVs**

AFVs are classified according to their characteristics and the role they play on the battlefield. There are numerous types of AFVs but they can be broadly classified into tanks, troop carriers, amphibious vehicles, armored engineering vehicles, air defense vehicles, and self-propelled artillery.

Tanks are classified by size and role, with the main battle tank, or universal tank, being the most popular model for modern warfare thanks to its high level of firepower, mobility, and protection. Troop carriers refer to vehicles designed to transport troops and can be divided into three main types: armored personnel carriers (APCs), infantry fighting vehicles (IFVs) and infantry mobility vehicles (IMVs). The main difference lies in their role. APCs are designed to transport and protect while IFVs also have offensive capabilities. Meanwhile, IMVs serve as patrol and security vehicles.

1. Which of the following is not an example AFVs?

   a) universal tank
   b) Infantry Fighting Vehicle
   c) armored engineering vehicles
   d) patrol car

2. What is the main difference between APCs and IFVs?

   a) The roles they play in the field are different.
   b) APCs have more firepower then IFVs.
   c) APCs are used more in patrol missions.
   d) IFVs are predominately security vehicles.

3. How are AFVs classified?

4. What does the passage mean by amphibious vehicles?

5. Why is the main battle tank the preferred model in modern warfare?

6. What do IFVs have that APCs don't?

## C  Grammar : Superlatives

| one of + the + superlative + plural noun | The FV101 Scorpion CVR is **one of the fastest** tanks in the world. |
| the + superlative + adjective clause | This tank is equipped with **the strongest armor** modern technology has to offer. |
| the + superlative + of all | The main battle tank is **the most popular** of all. |
| the least = opposite of the most | This has to be **the least effective** system I've ever seen. |

**Fill the in the blanks with the appropriate superlative.**

1. The Panzerkampfwagen VIII Maus ("Mouse") is (heavy) _____ AFV ever built.

2. The K2 Black Panther is considered one of (advanced) _____ tanks in the world.

**Use superlatives of the given words to make your own sentences. Share with your partner.**

| bad | large | valuable | dangerous | funny | complicated | cold |

Unit 6. Military Technology  69

## D Speaking

Answer the following questions with your partner then discuss your answers as a class.

- What kind of vehicles have you been on? Which was the most impressive?
- What kind of AFVs does your country possess?
- What do you think is the purpose of armored engineering vehicles?
- How effective do you think AFVs are in the battlefield?

## E Warm Up for Listening

Label the image with the correct words.

| turret | hatch | hull | track | main gun |

a.

b.

c.

d.

e.

## F Listening (TRACK 23)

Listen to a conversation between two people and answer the following questions.

**1. What is NOT a feature of the M1A2 Abrams?**

a) Halon firefighting system
b) Missiles
c) M256 cannon
d) M240 machine gun

**2. What is the Softkill active protection system?**

a) It is a part of the composite armor.
b) It is a separate blow-out compartment.
c) It is a piece of art.
d) It is a device that disables the guidance system of some missiles.

**Circle T if the statement is true and F if false. Correct the false statements to make them true. Compare your answers with your partner.**

3. The Softkill active protection system is cutting edge technology.    T / F

4. The halon firefighting system prevents fires in the crew compartment.    T / F

5. The main gun on the M1A2 Abrams fires 120mm rounds.    T / F

6. The M1A2 Abrams has four speeds.    T / F

# G Grammar : Preposition Combinations

Prepositions are often combined with adjectives to mean something specific. Work with a partner and fill in the gaps with the appropriate preposition to identify common preposition combinations.

| Phrasal Verb | Example |
|---|---|
| ex) be accustomed to | It takes a while to <u>get accustomed to</u> the new environment when you get deployed overseas. |
| | I am not afraid _____ anything! |
| | I need to get out of the house for a bit. My roommate is really angry _____ me. |
| | We need to apply _____ the visa ASAP. |
| | I need to concentrate _____ my target practice. |
| | A squad consists _____ two or three fireteams. |
| | The majority of casualties die _____ blood loss on the field. |
| | We disagree _____ most things. |
| | He escaped _____ the enemy camp. |
| | I'm not familiar _____ this model. |
| | He insists _____ commanding this mission himself. |
| | I'm so embarrassed. I feel like the whole squad is laughing _____ me. |
| | Our uniforms are made _____ extremely durable material. |
| | He was opposed _____ the idea. |
| | Anything could happen on this mission so you must be prepared _____ combat. |
| | You are responsible _____ your own gear when you're out on the field. |
| | I'm sick and tired _____ the food here! |
| | I'm worried _____ Smith. He seems really down. |

Unit 6. Military Technology 71

## H Speaking

**Answer the following questions with your partner then discuss your answers as a class.**

- What do you think is the most impressive piece of military technology? Why?
- What weapons do you think should be banned from international warfare? Why?
- How do you think the future of military technology will look like?

# Unit Wrap Up

**Write a paragraph about a weapon of your choice. Make sure to include:**

- why you chose the weapon
- when it was made and used in battle
- its features

**Present in front of your class and try not to refer to any notes. You may use visual aids.**

# Military Exercises

## LESSON 13:
## WAR GAMES

▶ **Lesson Objectives**

Upon completion of the lesson, you will be able to
» discuss military exercises
» accurately repeat a comparative
» accurately use double comparatives

**UNIT 7**

## A Warm Up for Reading

① What do you think is happening in the picture below? Why? Discuss with a partner.

② Fill in the blanks with the appropriate word.

| warfare | FTX | CPX | rehearsal | in tandem |
| --- | --- | --- | --- | --- |

a) To do something _____ means to do them at the same time.

b) A _____ is a practice run before the real event.

c) A _____ is a full-scale practice run of actual warfare.

d) _____ refers to military operations between enemies.

e) _____ focuses on preparing commanders for battle.

## B Reading  TRACK 24

**Military Exercises**

Military exercises or war games allow the military to study the effects of warfare and test war strategies without engaging in actual combat. It also ensures the combat readiness of deployable troops.

The four main types of exercises are Field Training Exercises (FTX), Command Post Exercises (CPX), simulations, and joint exercises. FTX are typically full-scale practice rehearsals for actual warfare. Exercise Valiant Shield, the largest war games of the U.S. since the Vietnam war, is an example of FTX. A CPX focuses on those in command and can be run in tandem with a FTX or as a stand-alone event. Simulations allow commanders to run through different scenarios when military planning by using models and computer simulations. As warfare becomes more and more complex, the need for simulations has increased. Finally, joint exercises refer to war games involving multiple armed forces or nations.

**1.** Which of the following are objectives of military exercises? (2 answers)

a) To study the cause of wars
b) To simulate war strategies
c) To make sure soldiers are ready for combat
d) To engage in actual combat

**2.** What type of military exercise would Operation Bright Star (a exercise led by the U.S. and Egyptian forces in Egypt) be?

a) FTX
b) CPX
c) Simulation
d) Joint exercise

**3.** What is a FTX?

**4.** What is a CPX?

**5.** What is a simulation?

**6.** What is a joint exercise?

## C Grammar : Repeating a Comparative

You can give the idea that something is getting progressively greater by repeating the same comparative.

> ex) Warfare is becoming **more and more** complex.
> The scale of modern FTXs are becoming **larger and larger**.

**Fill in the blanks with the appropriate repeating comparative from the box.**

| | | | | |
|---|---|---|---|---|
| | advanced | far | tense | strong |

1. We need to retreat! The enemy fire is getting _____.

2. Hurry! The target is getting _____ away!

3. Modern weapons are becoming _____ every day.

4. Relations between the two countries have become _____ in the last couple of years.

**Make your own sentences using repeating comparatives and share with your partner.**

_____

_____

## D Speaking

**Answer the following questions with your partner then discuss your answers as a class.**

- What military exercises do you know of?
- Have you ever participated in a military exercise? How was it? If not, what do you think a military exercise would be like?

## E Warm Up for Listening

**Fill in the blanks with the appropriate word.**

| | | | | |
|---|---|---|---|---|
| seize | secure | combat position | assault | passage of lines |

1. He was imprisoned for aggravated _____.

2. To _____ something means to take something suddenly and forcefully.

3. We need to keep this in a _____ place. It is very important.

4. Occupy a _____ and wait for my signal to engage.

5. A/an _____ is an operation in which a force moves to engage with enemy combatants.

Unit 7. Military Exercises

## F Listening (TRACK 25)

Listen to a conversation between two people and answer the following questions.

1. What is First Platoon's objective?
   a) Seize and secure the bridge
   b) Assault Objective Red 2
   c) Take out the mortar
   d) Assist B company

2. When will the mission begin?
   a) 9 hours from now
   b) 9 o'clock tonight
   c) 9 o'clock tomorrow night
   d) 9 o'clock tomorrow morning

Circle T if the statement is true and F if false. Correct the false statements to make them true. Compare your answers with your partner.

3. The objective of this mission is to gain control of the bridge.   T / F
4. Second will be positioned on the left and lead the assault.   T / F
5. Second Platoon will disable the mortar.   T / F
6. Third Platoon will gain control of the bridge.   T / F

## G Grammar : Double Comparatives

A double comparative has two parts that both start with **the**. The second part is the result of the first part of the comparison.

> ex) **The faster** we gain control of the bridge, **the better** our chances of winning.
> **The larger** the vehicle, **the slower** it is.

**Complete the sentences with double comparatives.**

> ex) If the technology is good, the tank is strong. ⇨ The better the technology, the stronger the tank.

1. If the assault is swift, our chances of victory are good.

   ......................................................................................................................................

2. The weapons are powerful. We should be careful.

   ......................................................................................................................................

3. If the mission is big, I get nervous.

   ......................................................................................................................................

**Make sentences of your own and share them with your partner.**

......................................................................................................................................

## H Speaking

Design a military exercise of your own and brief your partner. Make sure you include the objective, timeline, and roles of the participants.

# LESSON 14:
# MAP READING

**UNIT 7**
**Military Exercises**

▶ **Lesson Objectives**

Upon completion of the lesson, you will be able to
» read maps
» accurately give coordinates
» give the location of a feature relative to a point of reference

## A  Warm Up for Reading

**1** Label the images with the correct word.

| desert | mountain | jungle | arctic | urban |

a. ......................

b. ......................

c. ......................

d. ......................

e. ......................

**2** Using the words in exercise 1, guess what the reading passage will be about. Discuss with your partner.

## B Reading  TRACK 26

**Map Reading**

Maps are an essential part of military life. They feature the five main terrains (desert, mountain, jungle, artic, and urban) and depict the topographical features of an area. Maps are drawn to scale to accurately represent the terrain. Large scale maps are usually used for navigation and not only help soldiers identify the topography of the land, but also locate areas that could be used for protection and concealment. Small scale maps are frequently used for strategic planning since they show a broader area than large scale maps.

The military uses grid coordinates when locating things on maps. When reading coordinates, the horizontal grid number should be read first, followed by the vertical. It is also common to break each grid down into tenths and provide a six-digit grid location for more accurate position descriptions.

**1. Why are maps drawn to scale?**

a) To provide a realistic view of the actual terrain.
b) To make it easier to draw an accurate map.
c) To make large scale and small scale maps.
d) To accurately represent the area around base.

**2. What can be inferred about the large scale maps?**

a) It is usually used by commanders.
b) It shows a broad area.
c) It uses different colors for different terrains.
d) It shows terrain features in more detail than small scale maps.

**3. What are the five main terrains?**

**4. What kind of map would be used to find bridges in the area?**

**5. Which word in the passage refers to the act of hiding?**

**6. Which numbers out of the six-digit grid coordinates 125612 belong to the vertical grid?**

## C Grammar : Map Reading

When reading coordinates, **grid** is said first followed by the individual numbers.

> *ex) 175237 is read* **grid one seven five two three seven**.

When using four-figure reference, the first two numbers refer to the horizontal grid and the last two the vertical.

> *ex) There is a village at grid 1849*

When using six-figure reference, the first three numbers refer to the horizontal grid and the last three the vertical. Think of the third and sixth digits of the coordinates as decimal points.

*ex) There is a bridge at grid 171488*

**Find the features at these coordinates.**

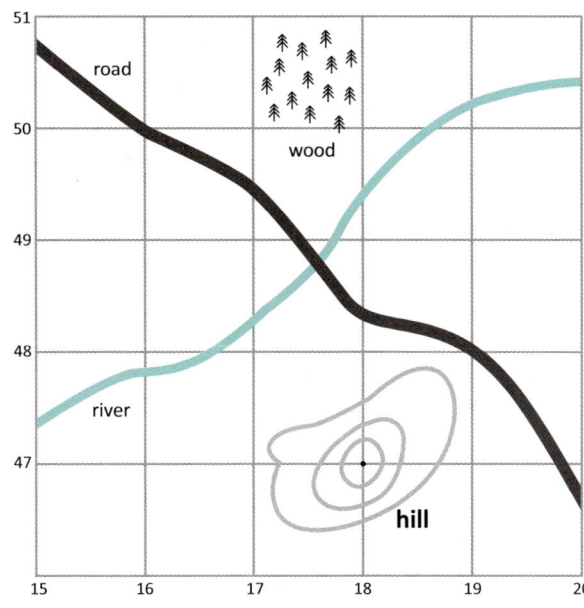

1. 158502

2. 174502

3. 1847

## D Speaking

**Work with a partner. Student A looks at image A and describes the map using coordinates. Student B draws the features student A mentions on image B. Change roles and work on images C and D.**

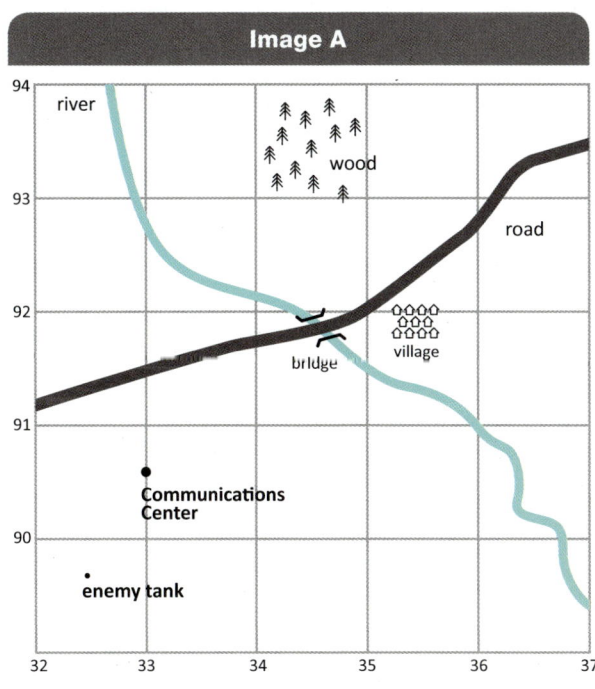

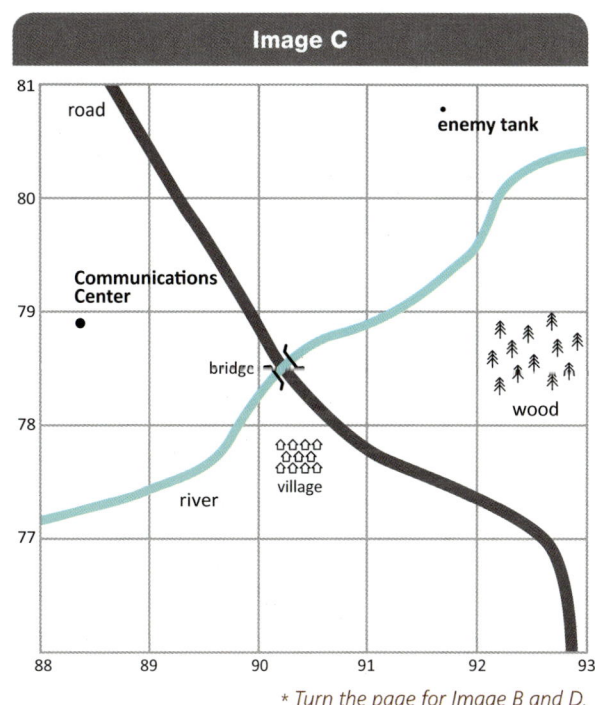

*\* Turn the page for Image B and D.*

Unit 7. Military Exercises  **79**

## Image B

## Image D

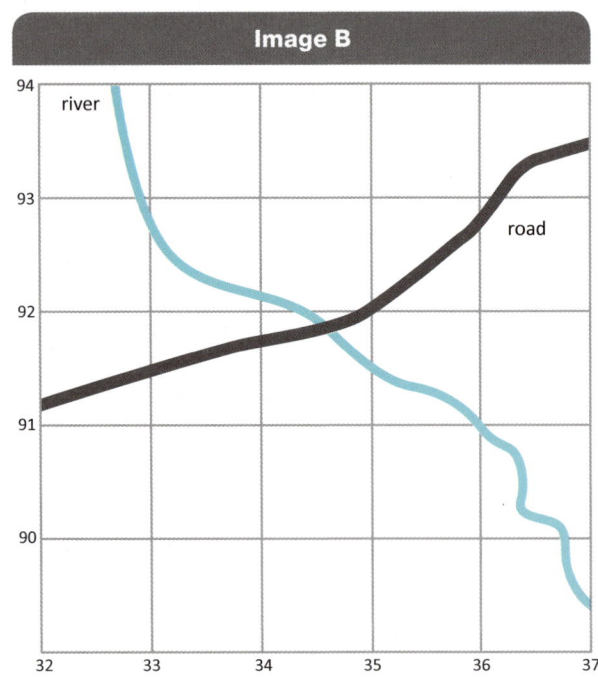

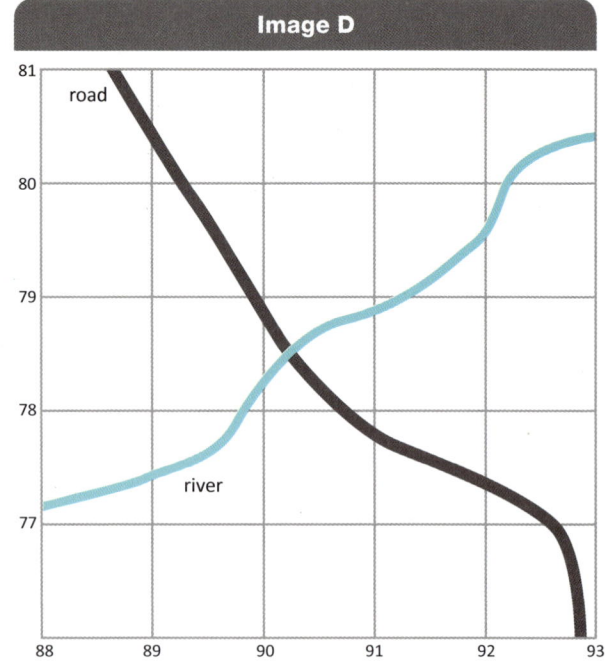

## E Warm Up for Listening

**Label the images with the correct word.**

hill saddle valley ridge depression

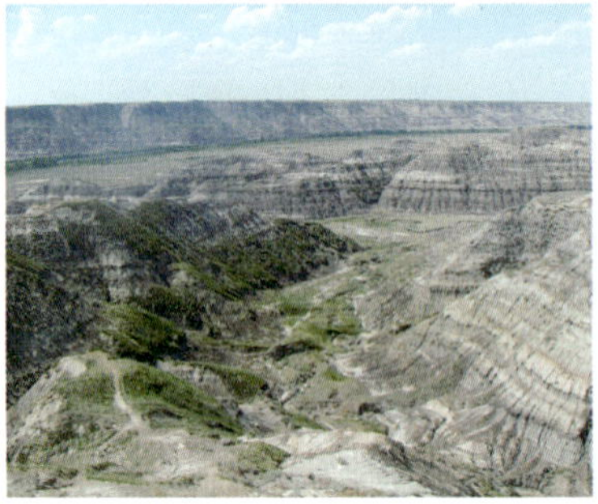

a. ______

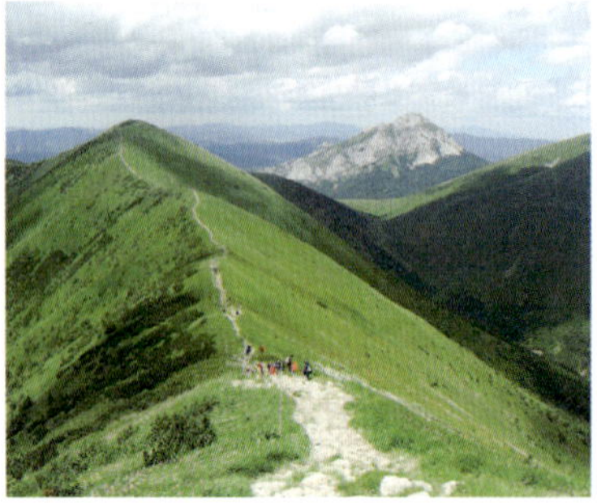

b. ______

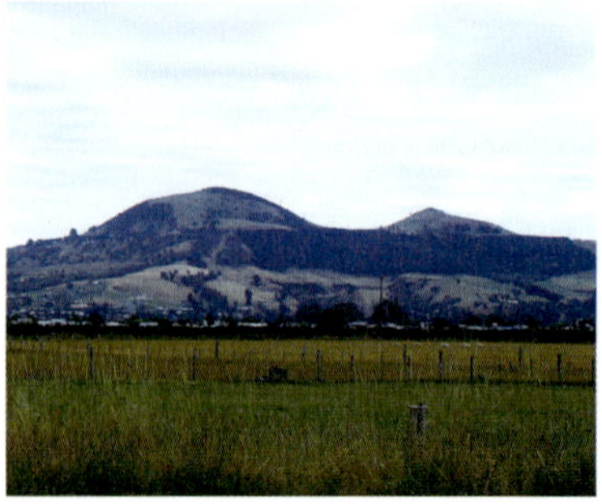

c. ______

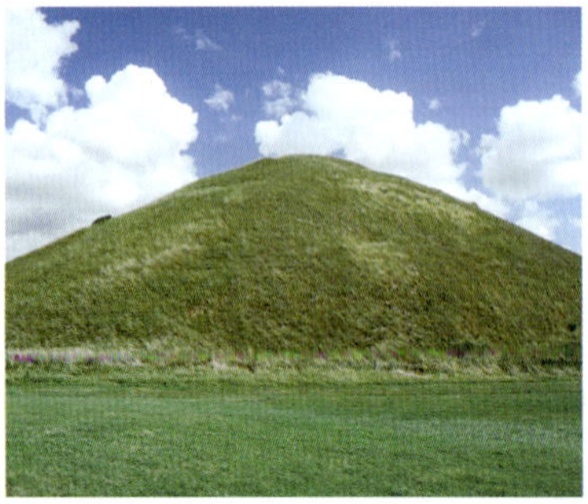

d. ______

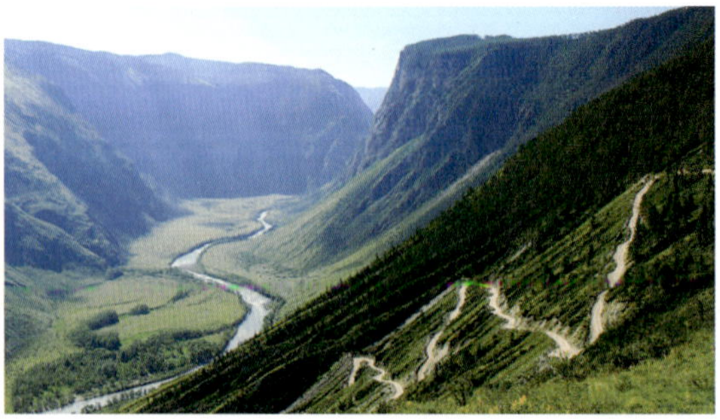

e. ______

## F Listening  TRACK 27

**Listen to a conversation between two people and answer the following questions.**

1. What is the squad's objective?
   a) To destroy the communications center
   b) To monitor the terrain
   c) Reconnaissance
   d) To destroy enemy forces

2. What should the platoons do about the enemy tank?
   a) Destroy it
   b) Nothing
   c) Avoid it
   d) Report it

**Label the map with the correct features from the box.**

| communications center | enemy | firing position | friendly forces |

3. ..................................
4. ..................................
5. ..................................
6. ..................................

## G Grammar : Location

The expression **in the vicinity of** can be used to express that something is close or to refer to a general area.

> ex) *There is a communications center* **in the vicinity of** *grid 1542.*

A location can be given with regards to a point of reference.

> ex) *Friendly forces are located about 15km south of the enemy tank.*
>         what              distance+direction of+point of reference

Unit 7. Military Exercises  81

**Use the expressions above to describe the location of the following features.**

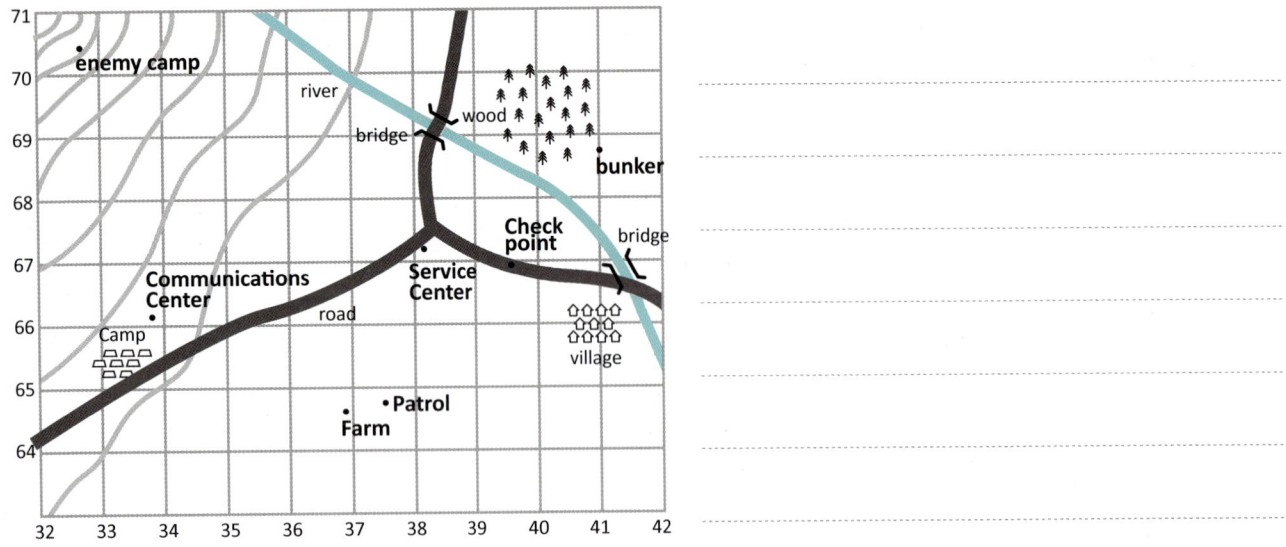

## H Speaking

Draw a map of your own and position at least 4 features on the map. Describe the map to your partner and see how accurately they can draw it.

# Unit Wrap Up

**Write a paragraph about a military exercise of your choice. Make sure to include:**

- why you chose the exercise
- who was involved and when it took place
- the social implications of the exercise

**Present in front of your class and try not to refer to any notes. You may use visual aids.**

# Convoys

## UNIT 8

### LESSON 15:
### CONVOYS

▶ **Lesson Objectives**

Upon completion of the lesson, you will be able to
» recognize and describe convoys
» accurately use non-action verbs
» accurately use participial adjectives

## A Warm Up for Reading

**1** Label the images with the correct word.

| convoy | medical aid | supplies | enemy assault |

a. ....................

b. ....................

c. ....................

d. ....................

**2** Using the words in exercise 1, guess what the reading passage will be about. Discuss with your partner.

## B Reading  TRACK 28

### Convoys

A convoy refers to a group of vehicles travelling together for mutual support and protection. The military forms a convoy when they need to move troops and supplies through various terrains.

Since a convoy entails numerous high-risk situations from driver fatigue to enemy assault, a risk management assessment is essential before every operation, where the anticipated course is physically inspected. Other potential hazards such as choke points and dangerous intersections must also be put into account when choosing a route. Once on the road, the convoy commander is responsible for the procession and for anticipating any danger the march column may encounter. They also organize regular halts for maintenance, supply checks and driver morale. The vehicle that leads the convoy is called the pacesetter and the last few, which are responsible for maintenance, recovery and medical aid, are the rear vehicles.

**1. Why does the military use convoys?**
   a) For mutual support and protection
   b) To avoid dangerous situations
   c) To safely move soldiers and supplies
   d) To keep in pace

**2. What is used to determine the convoy route?**
   a) Physical inspection
   b) Maintenance checks
   c) Risk management assessment
   d) Convoy schedule

**3.** Name at least 3 dangerous situations a convoy may face on the road.

.................................................................................................................................................

**4.** What role do the rear vehicles play?

.................................................................................................................................................

**5.** What is the role of the pacesetter?

.................................................................................................................................................

**6.** What are the reasons for a convoy to stop?

.................................................................................................................................................

## C Grammar : Non-action Verbs

Non-action verbs express a situation that exists, not one that is in progress. Therefore, they are not used in the progressive tense.

> ex) The military forms a convoy when they **need to** move troops and supplies. (O)
> The military forms a convoy when they **are needing to** move troops and supplies. (X)

| List of common non-action verbs | | | | | |
|---|---|---|---|---|---|
| be | forget | know | need | see | want |
| believe | hate | like | need | sound | |
| belong | have | love | prefer | think | |
| exist | hear | need | remember | understand | |

**Fill in the blanks with either the simple present or present progressive form of the verb in parentheses.**

**1.** Private Gomez. What can you see?
   I (look) .................................... towards where the enemy base is and I (see) .................................... a couple of vehicles approaching.

**2.** The enemy (approach) .................................... ! We (need) .................................... backup!

**3.** We (believe) .................................... the enemy (possess) .................................... at least 5 AFVs.

**Make your own questions and give them to your partner to solve.**

.................................................................................................................................................

.................................................................................................................................................

84 On the Job English _ Armed Forces 1

## D Speaking

Read the reading passage again and take notes of the main points. Tell your partner about convoys using your own words. You may include additional information from your own knowledge.

## E Warm Up for Listening

Fill in the blanks with the appropriate word.

| release point | ETA | march column | resistance | choke point |

1. A/an _____ is a very narrow road.

2. The _____ refers to the destination of a convoy.

3. _____ is the time a party is expected to arrive at a certain destination.

4. A/an _____ refers to the convoy formation.

5. _____ has a similar meaning to opposition.

## F Listening (TRACK 29)

Listen to a conversation between two people and answer the following questions.

1. What are the two speakers doing?

   a) Planning a convoy mission
   b) Talking about a past mission they were on
   c) Discussing the specific route of a convoy mission
   d) Discussing the potential threats of an upcoming convoy mission

2. What recommendation does the woman have for the threats mentioned by the man? (2 answers)

   a) Move quickly
   b) Be on the lookout for potential danger
   c) Have the rear vehicles be prepared for enemy fire
   d) Choose the route with caution

3. What is the objective of this mission?

4. How many hours will the whole movement take?

5. Why is the woman surprised that the commander is Captain Conway?

6. Why are they expecting resistance?

# G Grammar : Participial Adjectives

When used as an adjective, the past participle **(-ed)** describes how a person feels.

> ex) I'm just a little **surprised**.

When used as an adjective, the present participle **(-ing)** describes the cause of the feeling.

> ex) It's **surprising** that Captain Conway is the commander for this convoy.

**Fill in the blanks with either the *-ed* or *-ing* form of the word in parenthesis.**

1. The roads here can be extremely (confuse) _____. Be careful you don't take a wrong turn.
2. I was (alarm) _____ by the loud noise.
3. I'm absolutely (exhaust) _____. I've been driving all day.
4. Keep a close eye on the road. That noise just now is slightly (alarm) _____.

**Make 2 sentences each using the *-ed* and *-ing* form of the following words.**

| embarrass | shock | depress | interest | excite |
|---|---|---|---|---|

---
---
---
---
---

# H Speaking

**Answer the following questions with your partner then discuss your answers as a class.**

- What do you know about convoys? Have you ever been a part of one?
- What other dangers do you think a convoy could face?
- What are some famous convoy missions you have heard of?

# LESSON 16 :
# BRIEFINGS

**UNIT 8**
Convoys

▶ **Lesson Objectives**

Upon completion of the lesson, you will be able to
» give a briefing
» accurately use *get + adjective / past participle*

## A  Warm Up for Reading

**1** Label the images with the correct word.

| intersection | T-junction | roundabout | fork | bridge |

a. ..................................

b. ..................................

c. ..................................

d. ..................................

e. ..................................

**2** Using the words in exercise 1, guess what the reading passage will be about. Discuss with your partner.

Unit 8. Convoys  **87**

# B Reading  TRACK 30

**Convoy Briefing**

The start point is the gas station at grid 325672. You will join the humanitarian aid convoy here at 0700 hours and head north on the A6. It's a nice road but your trucks are slow so anticipate a maximum speed of 50km/h.

Go straight through the intersection and make a right at the T-junction. Continue on the B24 until you reach a service station on your right. This is your first stop and reporting point. You will be expected to report at 0800 hours.

After leaving the rest area, continue on the B24 until you come to a roundabout. Take the third exit sign-posted B27. Continue on the B27 and make a left at the fork. Once you get to the bridge, you'll know you're getting closer to the release point. Take the second right after the bridge. Your release point is the hospital on your right immediately after the turn. Your ETA is 0930 hours.

**1.** How long is the mission expected to last?

a) 1 hour
b) 1.5 hours
c) 2 hours
d) 2.5 hours

**2.** Where is their reporting point?

a) On the A6
b) Close to the T-junction
c) At the rest area
d) By the bridge

**Using the map below, write the right letter for the following locations.**

**3.** start point _____   **4.** reporting point _____   **5.** B27 _____   **6.** release point _____

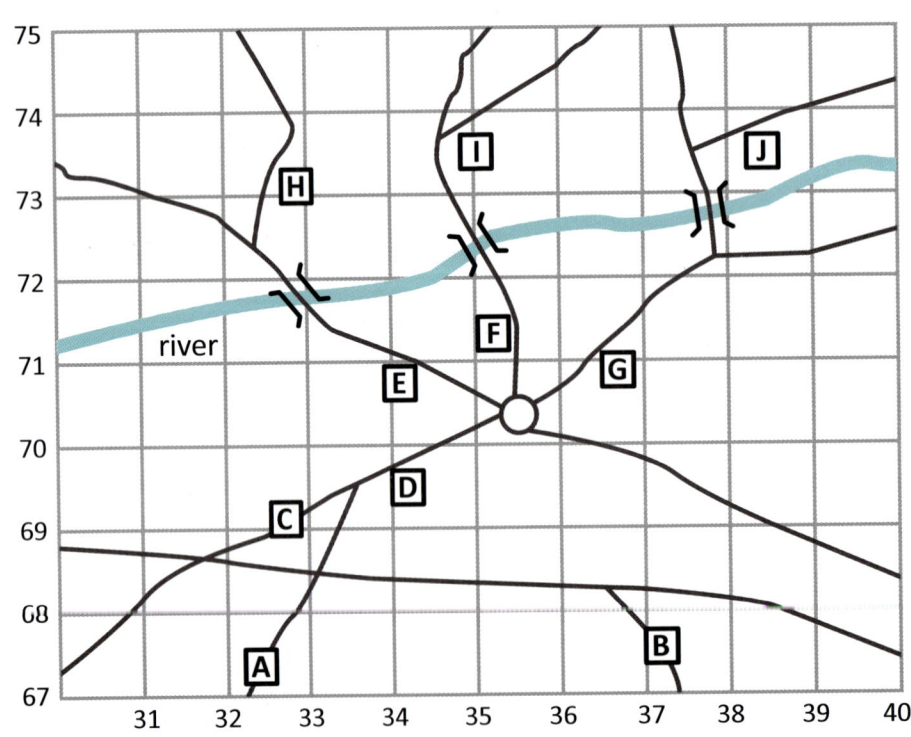

## C Grammar: Get + Adjective

Using **get** before an adjective gives the idea that something is changing or becoming to be like the adjective.

> ex) We are **getting closer** to the release point.
> I am **getting hungry**.

**Complete the sentences with the appropriate form of *get* and an adjective from the list.**

| sleepy | cold | sick | dark |
|---|---|---|---|

1. It's _____. I can't really see anything.
2. I think we should make a stop soon. The driver is _____.
3. It _____ after sundown in the desert.
4. I _____ after eating dinner yesterday.

**Make your own sentences using the following adjectives.**

| big | angry | dirty | dizzy | well |
|---|---|---|---|---|

_____

_____

_____

## D Speaking

**Use the following map and plan a convoy mission of your own. State the objective, ETA, starting point, release point and any rest areas and reporting points. Brief your partner on your mission and see if they can accurately pinpoint the locations and route on the map.**

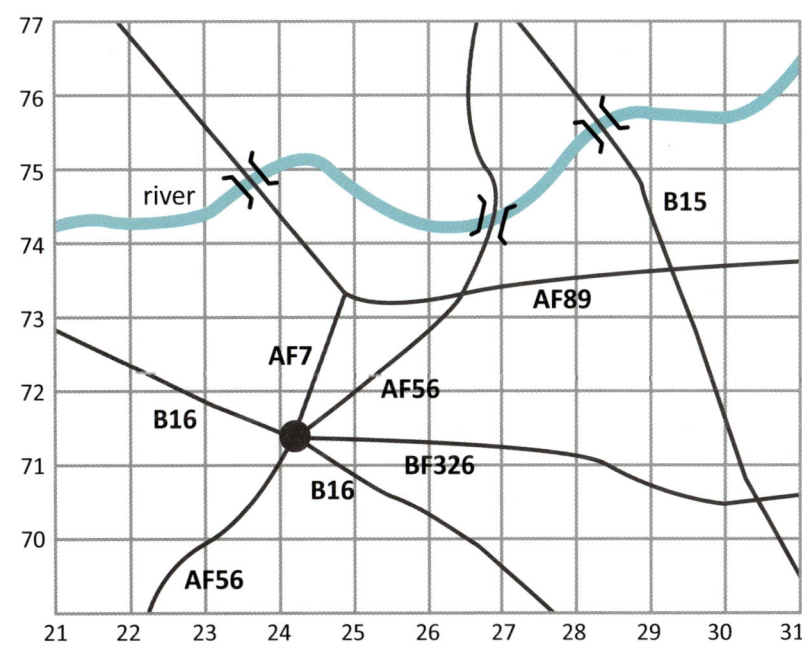

Unit 8. Convoys 89

## E   Warm Up for Listening

**Fill in the blanks with the appropriate word.**

| route | service station | strip | ambush |
|---|---|---|---|

1. A/an _____ refers to a facility that sells gas and has a repair garage.

2. We were blindsided! It was a/an _____ !

3. A/an _____ is a way or course to get from a starting point to a destination.

4. A/an _____ is a road or strip with a heavy density of businesses on either side.

## F   Listening   TRACK 31

**Listen to a conversation between two people and answer the following questions.**

1. Which of the following roads does the convoy NOT take?

   a) AF35
   b) AF56
   c) AF89
   d) B14

2. Why will the convoy not go above 40km/h?

   a) Because of the condition of the road
   b) Because the trucks in the convoy are slow
   c) Because they will go through enemy territory
   d) To avoid getting ambushed

**Circle T if the statement is true and F if false. Correct the false statements to make them true. Compare your answers with your partner.**

3. The starting point is grid 315907.   T / F

4. The movement will last 2.5 hours.   T / F

5. The first rest area will be 5 kilometers after the B14.   T / F

6. The strip on AF45 is controlled by enemy forces.   T / F

## G   Grammar : Get + Past Participle

A past participle after **get** describes the subject of the sentence, much like an adjective.

> ex) We have to be on high alert if we're going to avoid **getting ambushed**.
> You'd better be careful or you're going to **get hurt**.

**Complete the sentences with the appropriate form of *get* and a past participle from the list.**

| crowded | killed | lost | acquainted |
|---|---|---|---|

1. You two had better _____. You're going to be spending a lot of time together on the next mission.

2. Make sure you keep your eyes on the target. The square is _____.

3. I _____ because the roads were so confusing.

4. I heard they were forced to pull out because too many civilians were _____.

**Make your own sentences using the following past participles.**

| arrested | confused | drunk | invited |
|---|---|---|---|

........................................................................................................................................................

........................................................................................................................................................

........................................................................................................................................................

# H Speaking

**Work with a partner. Plan a convoy mission and draw the map. Brief another group and see if they can pinpoint the locations in the briefing.**

Unit 8. Convoys

# Unit Wrap Up

**Write a paragraph about this class. Include:**

- some of the things you learnt
- what you liked about it
- what you thought could be improved
- what surprised you about it

**Present in front of your class and try not to refer to any notes. You may use visual aids.**

# APPENDIX

1. LISTENING SCRIPTS
2. ANSWER KEY

On the Job English
**ARMED FORCES**

# 1. LISTENING SCRIPTS

## LESSON 1 : BASIC TRAINING

### F Listening  TRACK 2

| | |
|---|---|
| **Man** | Looks like we have a busy week ahead of us. Have you seen the schedule? |
| **Woman** | Yeah. I'm really looking forward to rappelling on Tuesday morning. |
| **Man** | Me too! But not so much the map reading in the afternoon. I've never really been good with maps. |
| **Woman** | Well you'd better pay attention this time or you know the sergeant will be all over you. Speaking of which, I think we have drill Monday morning? |
| **Man** | Yes, and nuclear biological and chemical defense training in the afternoon. |
| **Woman** | What about on Wednesday? |
| **Man** | I think it was first aid in the morning and communications training in the afternoon? |
| **Woman** | Ah! I remember now! No, it's the 5k tactical foot march in the morning. First aid training is on Thursday morning and weapons training in the afternoon. |
| **Man** | Well make sure you get some good sleep that night because we have a field training exercise on Friday and Saturday. |
| **Woman** | I know. Definitely not looking forward to that, I can tell you. |

## LESSON 2 : A MILITARY LIFE

### F Listening  TRACK 4

| | |
|---|---|
| **Man** | Hey Sarah! I haven't seen you in ages! How have you been? |
| **Woman** | Ben! I'm doing great thanks! |
| **Man** | I heard you enlisted a while back? |
| **Woman** | Yeah, a few months ago. I just got out of basic training. |
| **Man** | Wow! How was it? What was your day like? |
| **Woman** | Well, wake-up was at four thirty, which took some getting used to for sure! Then we had physical training from five for an hour. Then breakfast at seven for half an hour. |
| **Man** | Ugh! I don't think I'd be able to get up at half past four everyday let alone work out! So what were your mornings like? More PT? |
| **Woman** | No, thank God. We had classes from nine till noon. We'd get an hour for lunch, then back to class from one to five. Dinner was from six to seven. |
| **Man** | That sounds like a packed day. Did you ever have any time to just relax? |
| **Woman** | We had personal time in the evening from eight until nine so I'd usually read a book and unwind. Then it'd be lights out at nine. |

## LESSON 3 : RANK

### F Listening  TRACK 6

| | |
|---|---|
| **Sergeant Evans** | Sergeant Evans reporting, ma'am. |
| **Captain Thomas** | Good morning, Sergeant. At ease. |
| **Sergeant Evans** | You wanted to see me, ma'am? |
| **Captain Thomas** | Ah yes. How are the new recruits doing? I heard there was a problem during training? |
| **Sergeant Evans** | There was an altercation between a couple of the recruits and another was injured during the obstacle course but it isn't anything to be concerned about, ma'am. |
| **Captain Thomas** | Good, good. And I trust that preparations are underway for the field training exercise next weekend? |
| **Sergeant Evans** | Yes, ma'am. I have Corporal Smith working on the logistics and Corporal Bennings is overlooking the supplies. |
| **Captain Thomas** | Good. I actually asked to see you because the Colonel wants the list of the new recruits. Get it to me as soon as possible, please Sergeant. |
| **Sergeant Evans** | Right away, ma'am. |

## LESSON 4 : MILITARY ORGANIZATION

### F Listening  TRACK 8

| | |
|---|---|
| **Lieutenant Hart** | Lieutenant Hart reporting, sir. |
| **Captain Lone** | At ease, Lieutenant. |
| **Lieutenant Hart** | Lieutenant Phillips said you wanted to see me, sir? |
| **Captain Lone** | I have new orders to patrol area 34 and eliminate any threats, and I want second platoon on the mission. |
| **Lieutenant Hart** | Yes, sir. |
| **Captain Lone** | Who is in command of your squads, Lieutenant? |
| **Lieutenant Hart** | First squad is led by Corporal Robinson, second by Sergeant Oaks and Corporal Wrenn is in command of third, sir. |
| **Captain Lone** | Well for this mission, I want Corporal Stone in charge of second squad. |
| **Lieutenant Hart** | Yes, sir. |
| **Captain Lone** | Here are your platoon's orders. First squad will approach the area through hill 125. Once clear, second squad will set up a checkpoint at the base of the hill while third squad will be held in reserve. Is that understood? |

# 1. LISTENING SCRIPTS

| | |
|---|---|
| **Lieutenant Hart** | Yes, sir. Loud and clear. |
| **Captain Lone** | Good. Now, tell Sergeant Oaks I need to see him as soon as possible please, lieutenant. |
| **Lieutenant Hart** | Right away, sir. |

## LESSON 5 : ON POST

### F Listening  TRACK 10

| | |
|---|---|
| **Man** | What's our status on the MREs? |
| **Woman** | Not good. We're down to the last 10 cases. |
| **Man** | We need those A-rations ASAP. The MREs aren't going to last long. |
| **Woman** | Well I just talked to the platoon sergeant and I'm afraid it's a negative on getting them, any time soon. |
| **Man** | What? Why? |
| **Woman** | I'm not sure. Something about personnel being stretched thin on post. No one expected this mission to last this long. |
| **Man** | Did he say how long it would be until we got any? |
| **Woman** | He said anywhere between 3 days to a week. |
| **Man** | Well, what are our options? |
| **Woman** | We're going to have to rely on First Strike Rations until we get resupplied. |
| **Man** | We'd better make them last! |

## LESSON 6 : UNIFORM AND TACTICAL GEAR

### F Listening  TRACK 12

| | |
|---|---|
| **Woman** | Right. And now we're going to move on to packing your field gear. Pay attention because everything you need for your survival will be in this rucksack. As you can see, your MOLLE pack consists of a frame, shoulder straps, and a padded waistband. I trust you already know how to put it together? |
| **Man** | Yes, ma'am. |
| **Woman** | Good. Remember to pack your rucksack on the floor, horizontally. You don't want to risk injury on the field because the balance of the items inside is offset. |
| **Man** | Ma'am, then should we put the heavier items on the bottom? |
| **Woman** | Yes. You also want to put the heaviest items against the frame for maximum support. Remember, your full battle rattle is going to weigh about 50kg so distributing that weight as efficiently as possible is going to make a huge difference when you're on the field. |

| | |
|---|---|
| **Man** | Yes, ma'am. |
| **Woman** | And make sure to pack all the essentials: hydration sack, MREs, extra food and water… what else? |
| **Man** | Sun protection, fire kit, flashlight, sunglasses, and communication gear, ma'am. |
| **Woman** | Good. Next, you want to make sure to secure everything and tuck in any drawstrings. I'd also recommend attaching your first aid kit, some ammo pouches, and a flashlight to your TAP for easy access. |

## LESSON 7 : EXERCISE AND HEALTH

### F Listening  TRACK 14

| | |
|---|---|
| **Woman** | So how did you do on last week's PFT? |
| **Man** | I barely passed. I mean, I knew I was out of shape but I didn't think I'd do that bad! |
| **Woman** | Well you'd better start working out so you do better on the next one. |
| **Man** | Yeah. I think I did okay on the 2 mile run but it's the strength events I'm having trouble with. And more the push-ups than the sit-ups. I think my core is way stronger than my upper body. |
| **Woman** | Well hitting the gym a few times a week should fix that. |
| **Man** | Yeah, I guess. But to be honest, I'm more worried about the obstacle course coming up next week than the PFT. |
| **Woman** | What do you mean? I love the obstacle course! |
| **Man** | Yeah well that's because you're a workout fanatic. I just know I'm going to get stuck on the low wall again. And the cargo net is a pain too. Basically anything I have to heave myself over I'm not going to enjoy. The same goes for climbing out of the ditch. Running across the logs or jumping the fence isn't as bad as the others, but the absolute worst is crawling under the wire. |
| **Woman** | Oh stop being such a baby. The way I see it, you need to get in shape anyway and this is going to do nothing but help. |
| **Man** | Yeah, I guess you're right. I have to stop complaining and put on my big boy pants. |

## LESSON 8 : HEALTH AND FIRST AID

### F Listening  TRACK 16

| | |
|---|---|
| **Man** | Ok recruits. Listen up. What you learn today may save your or your friend's life so pay attention. First, let's start with the basics. What is first aid? Riley? |
| **Woman** | It's first care given to casualties before they can be seen by a medical professional, sir. |
| **Man** | Good. Remember, your goal is not to fix the patient. It is to make sure the casualty is breathing, stop any bleeding, help overcome shock, relieve pain, and prevent infections. There are three steps you should take to ensure the first of these happens; the ABC of medical treatment if you will. Does anyone know what that stands for? |

# 1. LISTENING SCRIPTS

**Woman**      Airway, breathing and circulation, sir.

**Man**      Right. So the first step is to open the airway and restore breathing. You want to tilt the person's head and lift their chin up like this, and make sure there is nothing obstructing their airways. If they aren't breathing, you should proceed to use CPR. Once breathing has been restored, you should stop any bleeding and protect wounds from infections.

**Woman**      Sir, can we use our own first aid dressing on a casualty?

**Man**      That's a negative. Always try to use the casualty's field dressing whenever possible. If the bleeding doesn't stop even after applying the dressing, you are going to have to apply manual pressure on the wound. Place a hand on the dressing and exert pressure for 5 to 10 minutes. You can get the patient to do it himself if he conscious and able. The next step is to prevent shock. Now, how can we tell if someone is going into shock?

**Woman**      They could have clammy or blotched or bluish skin, be nervous or confused, be nauseous or vomit, or pass out.

**Man**      People going into shock also tend to perspire freely. If you determine that your casualty is, indeed, going into shock, just remember PELCRN, that's P-E-L-C-R-N. Position on back, elevate legs, loosen clothing, climatize, reassure, and notify help.

## LESSON 9 : ON-BASE HOUSING

### F Listening  TRACK 18

**Man**      Well it's decided. They're going to have me stationed in Korea starting next year.

**Woman**      Well we've been expecting it for a while now so it's not exactly a surprise. It just means we have a lot of things to think over I guess.

**Man**      Yeah. I guess the first thing is, do we want the whole family to relocate or just me? I personally would like us all to move but I am a little concerned about the boys' school. And with another one on the way, I don't know how easy it would be to adapt to a completely new environment.

**Woman**      As long as we're on base, I don't think it would matter. The DoDEA schools are meant to be pretty good and as long as we have access to the community, I don't think there would be too much difficulty adjusting, language and culture wise. Do you know how much BAH we would get if we decided to live off base?

**Man**      I'm not sure. I'd have to look into it but I don't think I'd feel comfortable living off base to be honest.

**Woman**      Ok. Well we'd better hand in our paperwork as soon as possible then. I don't want to have to be put on a waiting list.

**Man**      I'll get that done as soon as I can. We're going to have to think about throwing out some of our stuff too. Maybe we could give some of it away?

**Woman**      Yeah. The Browns are coming over later so I'll ask if they want any of the boys' old stuff, and I could donate some things to the charity drive next week. Oh and this time, we're hiring someone to clean up. The last time we had to clean when we moved out was an absolute nightmare!

**Man**      Ok. I'll figure something out, don't worry.

## LESSON 10 : GETTING AROUND BASE

### F Listening  TRACK 19

| | |
|---|---|
| **Man** | Man, I'm so bored! There's nothing to do on base and I'm sick and tired of the dining room food! |
| **Woman** | Well, we could always go out. There's a really good Indian restaurant on Wood Street by Greenlanders Park. |
| **Man** | Nah, I don't like Indian. How about that Greek restaurant across from the post office? I heard they're giving discounts for service members this week. |
| **Woman** | There's a Greek joint by the post office? I thought that was where the pub was. |
| **Man** | Oh yeah! Sorry, the Greek joint is on Juniper Street right before you hit Engle Avenue. |
| **Woman** | Is that the one next to the pharmacy? |
| **Man** | Yup. |
| **Woman** | Ok. I've been wanting to go there anyway. I've heard good things about that place. And since we'll be out anyway, would you mind going to the shoe store with me? I need to get a pair of sneakers. |
| **Man** | Sure. Let's go to Shoes R Us. They have a really good collection. |
| **Woman** | I don't think I've been there before… where is it? |
| **Man** | It's pretty close to the restaurant. You just have to make a right on Wood Street and walk past W Federal Street and it's on your left. |

## LESSON 11 : HISTORY OF MILITARY TECHNOLOGY

### F Listening  TRACK 21

| | |
|---|---|
| **Man** | The armored fighting vehicle or AFV is a product of man's desire to combine mobility with both offensive and defensive capabilities. The concept predates the invention of the internal combustion engine, and sketches of a rudimentary tank by Leonardo da Vinci have been discovered dating back to 1485. Nowadays, AFVs can be classified depending on their type and role, but the main objective remains the same now as it did in ancient times: to provide troops with both mobile protection and firepower. Now, does anyone know what the first AFV was? |
| **Woman** | The armored cars used during WWI? |
| **Man** | Those could be considered the first modern AFVs, yes, but believe it or not, armored siege engines such as battering rams and trebuchets were actually the first examples of AFVs in history. |
| **Woman** | I'm sorry, sir, but aren't they a little too rudimentary to be called AFVs? I mean, they had to be manually lifted or pushed to be moved! |
| **Man** | You're right, but they eventually became the blueprint for mortars and artilleries, some of the most effective and destructive weapons we have today! The war wagons used in the 15th century are also a good example of primitive AFVs. These were wagons with protective sides, equipped with firepower such as cannons. It wasn't until the 20th century, WWI in fact, that tanks, as we know them today, were developed. There are many impressive things about the tank, but the thing I find most impressive is the speed at which it was developed. |

# 1. LISTENING SCRIPTS

|  | The initial design, Little Wille, was developed September 1915 and after a few improvements, the design for the prototype of the first actual tank was adopted in January 1916. And from then, it only took eight months to roll out the first tanks in the Battle of the Somme. |
|---|---|
| **Woman** | But sir, isn't the Renault FT light tank considered the standard for most modern tanks? |
| **Man** | That's right! It was also developed in 1916 by the French. Does anyone know why this particular model is considered the predecessor to the modern tank? |
| **Woman** | I believe it's the traversable turret and the engine in the back? |
| **Man** | Looks like someone's been doing their homework! |

## LESSON 12 : MODERN MILITARY TECHNOLOGY

### F Listening  TRACK 23

| **Woman** | Right. Here is our main battle tank, the M1A2 Abrams. It's one of the heaviest main battle tanks in service, weighing in at almost 68 short tons. So it goes without saying, you need to know what you're doing when operating this beauty. It has a multi-fuel turbine engine situated here, and it has a separate blow-out compartment for ammo storage. In addition to its composite armor, it also has a state of the art Softkill active protection system. Does anyone know what that is? |
|---|---|
| **Man** | It's a Missile Counteractive Device that can render the guidance of some missiles useless, ma'am. |
| **Woman** | That's right. It also has a halon firefighting system that automatically extinguishes fires in the crew compartment. Now pay close attention because you're going to need to familiarize yourselves with these parts. The main gun on the M1A2 Abrams is the M256 cannon. Does anyone know what rounds this model fires? |
| **Man** | I believe it fires 120mm rounds, ma'am. |
| **Woman** | Good. The gun's angle is controlled by the turret which, as you should all know, is able to rotate a full 360 degrees. The Abrams tank also has three machine guns, with an optional fourth. You can see the M2HB here, in front of the commander's hatch, and the M240 here, in front of the loader's hatch. The second M240 is to the right of the main gun. What do we call the exterior here? |
| **Man** | The hull ma'am. It's where the crew is housed. |
| **Woman** | And these? |
| **Man** | The tracks. It's what propels the tank forward. |
| **Woman** | Right. And it propels the tank at speeds of up to approximately 70 kilometers per hour on paved roads and 50 cross-country, so not too shabby. Does anyone know how many speeds it has? No one? It has four forward and two in reverse, so six in total. Since we're on the topic, why don't we take a look at the driving controls? |

## LESSON 13 : WAR GAMES

### 🇫 Listening  TRACK 25

| | |
|---|---|
| **Man** | Alright, so here are your orders for the FTX. The objective is to seize and secure the bridge. I want First, Second, and Third Platoons on this mission. Is that clear? |
| **Woman 1** | Yes, sir! |
| **Man** | First Platoon you will move forward first and occupy a combat position on the right. Your mission is to assault Objective Red 1 and suppress enemy machine gun fire so that B company can conduct a passage of lines through our position. Is that understood? |
| **Woman 1** | Yes, sir! |
| **Man** | And who is in command of Second Platoon? |
| **Woman 1** | Lieutenant Carter, Sir. |
| **Man** | Lieutenant Carter, your Platoon you will move forward after First Platoon and occupy a combat position on the left. Your mission is to destroy Objective Red 2 and assist C company with their passage of lines. Thirds Platoon will move in last and occupy a combat position between Second Platoon and First Platoon. Your job will be to seize and secure the bridge. The mission will commence at 0900 hours tomorrow and you will take this route to secure your positions. It looks as though the enemy doesn't have any AFVs but they do have a mortar. Second Platoon, it will be your job to disable it. Is that clear? |
| **Woman 2** | Yes, sir! |
| **Man** | Remember, the faster we gain control of the bridge, the better our chances of winning. |

## LESSON 14 : MAP READING

### 🇫 Listening  TRACK 27

| | |
|---|---|
| **Man** | The squad will begin the mission at grid 295695 and proceed west to grid 269687. There is a communications center in the vicinity. They will monitor the terrain and move south to grid 267679 once certain the area is secure. There have been reports of enemy activity in this area so their objective will be to survey the area and locate the enemy forces. They will move to grid 256661, making sure to remain in the cover of the saddle. The enemy is most likely to be located here. |
| **Woman** | Do you mean here at grid 254658? |
| **Man** | That's right. Once the enemy's position is verified, we will move in for the assault. |
| **Woman** | How many platoons do you think we'll need? |
| **Man** | Three. First Platoon will execute the assault, Second Platoon will provide security for the flanks and Third Platoon will be the reserve. We will approach the enemy from hill 135 at grid 248677. First Platoon will be at the front, Second Platoon in the middle and Third Platoon at the rear. At grid 253660, First and Second Platoons will secure the attack and firing position while Third Platoon protects the rear. |
| **Woman** | What about the tank? There are reports that an enemy tank is moving near grid 249658. |
| **Man** | The friendly forces located 15km south of there will take care of that. |

# 1. LISTENING SCRIPTS

## LESSON 15 : CONVOYS

### F Listening  TRACK 29

| | |
|---|---|
| **Man** | The mission of this convoy is to move the supplies from HQ to the release point, and to provide protection for the humanitarian aid vehicles. |
| **Woman** | When are we leaving and what's our ETA? |
| **Man** | We will leave HQ at 0600 hours and are estimated to arrive at 1300 hours. |
| **Woman** | Understood. Who is the commander? |
| **Man** | Captain Conway. |
| **Woman** | Captain Conway? |
| **Man** | Affirmative. Is there a problem? |
| **Woman** | No, no. I'm just a little surprised. I assumed it would be Captain Cruise. Anyway, how big is the convoy? |
| **Man** | There will be twenty vehicles in the march column. |
| **Woman** | Should we expect any resistance? |
| **Man** | Affirmative. We'll be passing through enemy territory so the commander is going to have to be on the lookout for any potential danger. There are also going to be numerous choke points within the city so we're going to have to choose the route with caution and move fast. |
| **Woman** | Understood. We'll have to make sure the pacesetter moves at a swift pace and the rear vehicles are ready in case of an attack. |

## LESSON 16 : BRIEFINGS

### F Listening  TRACK 31

| | |
|---|---|
| **Man** | Okay. So here's the brief for the convoy's route. We will leave HQ at 1300 hours and link up with the aid trucks at the service station at grid 315907. We will continue down the AF89 for approximately 50 kilometers. Keep in mind that the road is in poor condition so the convoy will maintain a maximum speed of 40km/h. Our first checkpoint will be at the roundabout at the junction with B14. We will take the first exit and continue on the B14 for 5 kilometers. Our first rest area will be at the service station on the left. After the 30 minute stop, we will continue on the B14 and make a right and take the AF56 at the intersection. We will continue along for 30 kilometers and cross the bridge. Our second rest area and checkpoint will be 1 kilometer from the bridge. After leaving the rest area, we will continue on the AF56 for 10 kilometers. This strip is territory controlled by enemy forces so we're going to have to be on high alert if we're going to avoid getting ambushed. Once we reach the roundabout, we will take the third exit and continue on the AF45 for 3 kilometers until we reach the release point on the left. Our ETA is 1630 hours. |

# 2. ANSWER KEY

## LESSON 1 : BASIC TRAINING

### A Warm Up for Reading

1. a. barracks
   b. first aid
   c. obstacle course
   d. recruits
   e. drill sergeant

### B Reading

1. d
2. c
3. F – Weapons training is conducted in the second phase
4. F – The recruits need to pass the final PT test to graduate
5. T
6. F – There is a PT test in the blue phase. The obstacle course is in the white phase.

### C Grammar : Adjective Clauses using *which* and *that*

1. The training, which (that) lasts for 10 weeks, transforms civilians into soldiers.
2. The barracks, which (that) are assigned at the beginning of training, are very clean.
3. The third phase, which is the most challenging (one), is the blue phase.

### E Warm Up for Listening

1. a. weapons training
   b. rappelling
   c. map reading
   d. foot march

### F Listening

1. a
2. b
3. drill
4. map reading
5. 5k tactical foot march
6. weapons training

### G Grammar : Prepositions of Time

1. at
2. in
3. on

## LESSON 2 : A MILITARY LIFE

### A Warm Up for Reading

1. 1:30 a.m. – 0130 – zero one thirty
   4:00 a.m. – 0400 – zero four hundred
   11:00 a.m. – 1100 – eleven hundred
   6:15 p.m. – 1815 – eighteen fifteen
   9:32 p.m. – 2132 – twenty one thirty two

### B Reading

1. d
2. a
3. To advertise (encourage shopping at the PX) / To notify changes to operating hours
4. 24 hours
5. 2 weeks
6. 9 p.m.

### C Grammar : Expressing Future Time

**Possible answers**

1. A : When are you going to / will you visit your parents?
   B : I'm going to visit them at Christmas.
2. A : What are you going to / will you have for dinner?
   B : I'm going to order some pizza.
3. A : Are you going to / Will you do anything special for your birthday?
   B : I'll probably just hang out with a few friends.

### E Warm Up for Listening

a. PT

# 2. ANSWER KEY

b. classes
c. personal time
d. lights out

### F Listening

1. a
2. b
3. wake-up
4. Physical Training (PT)
5. 0700-0730
6. 1200-1300
7. lights out

### G Grammar : Past habit – would / used to / past simple

1. was
2. used to be / was
3. would go / used to go / went
4. a. I heard you enlisted a while back? (no change)
   b. I just got out of basic training. (no change)
   c. What was your day like? / What did your day used to be like? / What would your day be like?
   d. Wakeup was / would be / used to be at four thirty.
   e. We had / would have / used to have / physical training from five for an hour.
   f. What were your mornings like? / What would your mornings be like? / What did your morning used to be like?
   g. We had / used to have / would have classes from nine till noon.
   h. We would get / used to get / got an hour for lunch.
   i. Dinner was / would be / used to be / from six to seven.
   j. Did you ever have any time just to relax? / Would you ever have time just to relax? / Did you ever used to have any time just to relax?
   k. We had / would have / used to have personal time in the evening.
   l. I would usually / used to / read a book and unwind.
   m. It would be / used to be / was lights out at nine.

## LESSON 3 : RANK

### A Warm Up for Reading

1. a. Corporal
   b. First Lieutenant
   c. Major General
   d. Colonel
   e. Sergeant

### B Reading

1. c
2. b
3. T
4. F – rank is not determined by experience (Senior NCOs rank lower than junior commissioned officers but have more experience)
5. T
6. F – The majority of people in the army are enlisted personnel.

### C Grammar : Present Perfect

1. Have you ever ridden a fighter jet?
   ⇨ Yes, I have / No, I haven't
2. Have you ever won something for free?
   ⇨ Yes, I have / No, I haven't
3. Have you ever traveled with your parents?
   ⇨ Yes, I have / No, I haven't
4. Have you ever been lost?
   ⇨ Yes, I have / No, I haven't

### E Warm Up for Listening

a. list
b. altercation
c. at ease
d. salute

### F Listening

1. b
2. a, c
3. Because she asked to see him

4. The logistics in the field training exercise
5. Overlooking the supplies for the field training exercise
6. Get the list of the new recruits

### G Grammar: Addressing Superiors and Subordinates Possible Answers

1. A : Corporal Tanner, I need the list of the recruits as soon as possible, please.
   B : Right away, sir.
2. A : Good morning, sir.
   B : Good morning, Staff.
3. A : Ah, Lieutenant Watson, just the man I wanted to see.
   B : Yes, sir?
4. A : Sergeant Major, you wanted to see me?
   B : Specialist Jenkins, please come in.

## LESSON 4 : MILITARY ORGANIZATION

### A Warm Up for Reading

a. company
b. platoon
c. division
d. fireteam
e. battalion

### B Reading

1. d
2. o
3. fireteam
4. corporal or sergeant
5. battalion
6. 10,000-20,000

### C Grammar: The Passive

1. A hierarchical structure is used by the modern day military because of efficiency.
2. A platoon is commanded by a lieutenant.
3. The order must be signed off by the colonel.

### E Warm Up for Listening

1. command
2. squad
3. patrol
4. checkpoint

### F Listening

1. c
2. d
3. Corporal Robinson
4. held in reserve
5. the base of the hill
6. Tell Sergeant Oaks that the captain wants to see him/her.

### G Grammar: Reported Speech

1. Captain Lone said (that) he/she wanted to see Lieutenant Hart as soon as possible.
2. Lieutenant Hart said (that) Corporal Stone was going to be in command of second squad.
3. Sergeant Oaks said (that) he had commanded second squad in Alpha company.

## LESSON 5 : ON POST

### A Warm Up for Reading

1. a. post office
   b. dining hall
   c. command center
   d. billets

### B Reading

1. a
2. b
3. F – a billet is a form of housing for the soldiers
4. T

Appendix 105

# 2. ANSWER KEY

5. F – Garrison rations and A-rations much be prepared
6. F – most posts have a PX

### C Grammar : Connecting Ideas

1. so
2. or
3. but
4. and / or

### E Warm Up for Listening

a. MRE
b. A-ration
c. First Strike Rations
d. case

### F Listening

1. c
2. b
3. 10 cases
4. 3 days to a week
5. First Strike Rations
6. The Platoon Sergeant

### G Grammar : Had Better

**Possible Answers**

1. You'd better set up a savings account otherwise you're not going to have any money saved up at all.
2. You'd better see the doctor before it gets any worse.
3. You'd better hurry or you're not going to be able to go and see your family.
4. We'd better reserve ASAP or we're going to miss out!

## LESSON 6 : UNIFORM AND TACTICAL GEAR

### A Warm Up for Reading

1. a. ACU
   b. camouflage
   c. flask

d. ASU
e. rucksack

### B Reading

1. A
2. C
3. formal dress
4. Army Combat Uniforms (ACUs) / field uniforms
5. pouch
6. MOLLE

### C Grammar : Since and For

Answers will vary.

### E Warm Up for Listening

a. shoulder straps
b. hydration sack
c. frame
d. communication gear

### F Listening

1. C
2. C
3. T
4. F – heavier items should be packed first
5. F – full combat gear weighs approximately 50kg
6. F – Ammo should be kept on the vest (TAP) for easy access

### G Grammar : Gerunds and Infinitives

Answers will vary.

## LESSON 7 : EXERCISE AND HEALTH

### A Warm Up for Reading

1. a. push-ups
   b. pull-ups
   c. swimming

d. 2 mile run

e. sit-ups

### B Reading

1. a
2. a, c
3. F – A score of at least 60 on each event is a pass
4. F – soldiers must take the APFT at least twice a year
5. T
6. F – some soldiers choose to swim

### C Grammar : Frequency Expressions (How often)

Answers will vary.

### E Warm Up for Listening

a. ditch
b. fence
c. wire
d. cargo net
e. low wall

### F Listening

1. d
2. d
3. the 2 mile run
4. because she is a workout fanatic / because she like to work out / because she is in great shape
5. low wall, cargo net, ditch
6. wire

### G Grammar : Comparisons

Answers will vary.

## LESSON 8 : HEALTH AND FIRST AID

### A Warm Up for Reading

1. a. tourniquet
   b. gauze
   c. surgical gloves
   d. first aid kit
   e. bandage

### B Reading

1. b
2. a
3. T
4. T
5. T
6. T

### C Grammar : Reflexive Pronouns

1. yourself
2. himself

3-5. Answers will vary

### E Warm Up for Listening

a. pass out
b. field dressing
c. CPR
d. infection

### F Listening

1. C
2. D
3. when the casualty is not breathing
4. the casualty's field dressing
5. clammy, blotched, or bluish skin / nervous/ confused / nauseous / vomit / pass out
6. position on back, elevate legs, loosen clothing, climatize, reassure, notify help

### G Grammar : Modal Auxiliaries can and may

1. may / might / could - possibility
   can - ability
2. can't - ability
   can - ability

# 2. ANSWER KEY

3. may not / cannot / can't - permission
4. may / might / could - possibility

## LESSON 9 : ON-BASE HOUSING

### A Warm Up for Reading

1. Answers will vary
2. a. paycheck
   b. utilities
   c. on-base housing
   d. allowance
   e. service member

### B Reading

1. d
2. b, d
3. T
4. T
5. F – on base housing is limited so they may have to wait up to a year
6. F – the quality of the houses vary

### C Grammar : Phrasal Verbs

**Possible Answers**

| Phrasal Verb | Type |
|---|---|
| break down | I |
| Meaning | Example |
| stop functioning properly | My car broke down. |

| Phrasal Verb | Type |
|---|---|
| depend on | N |
| Meaning | Example |
| rely on | The BAH amount depends on 3 things. |

| Phrasal Verb | Type |
|---|---|
| call off | S |
| Meaning | Example |
| cancel | We're going to have to call off the event due to the weather. |

| Phrasal Verb | Type |
|---|---|
| find out about | N |
| Meaning | Example |
| discover information | When did you find out about your promotion? |

| Phrasal Verb | Type |
|---|---|
| get along with | N |
| Meaning | Example |
| have a good relationship with | I'm not getting along with my roommate. |

| Phrasal Verb | Type |
|---|---|
| get over | N |
| Meaning | Example |
| recover from an illness or a shock | He's just getting over a cold. |

| Phrasal Verb | Type |
|---|---|
| give up | I |
| Meaning | Example |
| quit doing (something) or quit trying | A soldier never gives up! |

| Phrasal Verb | Type |
|---|---|
| go over to | N |
| Meaning | Example |
| approach, visit another's home | I'm going over to Daniel's for dinner. |

### E Warm Up for Listening

1. DoDEA schools
2. paperwork
3. throw (them) out
4. think (it) over
5. relocate

### F Listening

1. b
2. d
3. Korea / next year

4. the school and the community
5. so they don't have to be put on a waiting list / so they can get a house without waiting
6. give them away to the Browns / give them to charity

## G Grammar : Phrasal Verbs

**Possible Answers**

| Phrasal Verb | Type |
|---|---|
| help out | S |
| **Meaning** | **Example** |
| assist | I help out at the children's home on the weekends. |

| Phrasal Verb | Type |
|---|---|
| point out | S |
| **Meaning** | **Example** |
| call attention to | He pointed out the mistakes in my report. |

| Phrasal Verb | Type |
|---|---|
| put off | S |
| **Meaning** | **Example** |
| postpone | Let's put off going out for a couple of days. |

| Phrasal Verb | Type |
|---|---|
| run into | N |
| **Meaning** | **Example** |
| meet by chance | I ran into Private Conner the other day. |

| Phrasal Verb | Type |
|---|---|
| watch out for | N |
| **Meaning** | **Example** |
| be careful | Watch out for the stairs! |

| Phrasal Verb | Type |
|---|---|
| write down | S |
| **Meaning** | **Example** |
| write a note on a piece of paper | Let me just get a pen to write that down. |

| Phrasal Verb | Type |
|---|---|
| clean up | S |
| **Meaning** | **Example** |
| make neat and clean | Can you help me clean up? This place is a mess! |

| Phrasal Verb | Type |
|---|---|
| drop in on | N |
| **Meaning** | **Example** |
| visit without calling first or without an invitation | I'm going to drop in on Harry after work. He looked upset. |

| Phrasal Verb | Type |
|---|---|
| figure out | S |
| **Meaning** | **Example** |
| find the solution to a problem | Let me figure out the logistics. |

## LESSON 10 : GETTING AROUND BASE

### A Warm Up for Reading

1. on the corner of
2. next to
3. opposite
4. between
5. on the right

### B Reading

1. I – Fitness Center
2. G – Dental Clinic
3. C – Cinema
4. B – Grand Hotel
5. A – Anthony's Pizza
6. D – Chapel
7. E – PX
8. F – Pharmacy
9. H – Post Office
10. J – Bowling Ally

# 2. ANSWER KEY

### C Grammar: Count and Uncountable Nouns

1. mistake, pencil, doughnut, diamond, chair, cup, letter, patient, river, lake
2. storms
3. Gold / is / silver
4. help
5. is / food / refrigerators

### E Warm Up for Listening

1. hit
2. sick and tired
3. sale
4. go out

### F Listening

1. b, d
2. d
3. Greek restaurant
4. Pharmacy
5. Indian restaurant
6. Shoes R Us
7. Pub

### G Grammar: Articles

1. a
2. the
3. X
4. a
5. X
6. X

## LESSON 11: HISTORY OF MILITARY TECHNOLOGY

### A Warm Up for Reading

1. a. machine gun
   b. partisan
   c. cannon
   d. atomic bomb
   e. helicopter

### B Reading

1. b
2. a
3. F – it was used for the first time in 1893
4. F – the prototype was built in 1907
5. T
6. T

### C Grammar: Present Perfect Progressive

1. are using / have been using
2. are driving / have been trying
3. have been working on

4-5. Answers will vary.

### E Warm Up for Listening

a. tank
b. mortar
c. trebuchet
d. battering ram

### F Listening

1. a
2. c (1915) – a – d (January, 1916) – b (September, 1916)
3. predates
4. armored siege engines
5. rudimentary
6. traversable

### G Grammar: Past Perfect

1. 1-b
   2-a
2. 1-b
   2-a

# LESSON 12 : MODERN MILITARY TECHNOLOGY

## A  Warm Up for Reading

1. a. amphibious vehicle
   b. troop carrier
   c. artillery
   d. air defense vehicle

## B  Reading

1. d
2. a
3. according to their characteristics and their role / tanks, troop carriers, amphibious vehicles, armored engineering vehicles, air defense vehicles, self-propelled missiles
4. a vehicle that can operate on both land and water
5. because of its superior firepower, mobility and protection
6. offensive capabilities

## C  Grammar : Superlatives

1. the heaviest
2. the most advanced
3. answers will vary

## E  Warm Up for Listening

a. track
b. main gun
c. hatch
d. turret
e. hull

## F  Listening

1. b
2. d
3. T
4. F – it extinguishes fires that may occur in the crew compartment
5. T
6. F – it has 6 total, 4 forward and 2 in reverse

## G  Grammar : Preposition Combinations

| Phrasal Verb | Example |
|---|---|
| be accustomed to | It takes a while to get accustomed to the new environment when you get deployed overseas. |
| be afraid of | I am not afraid of anything! |
| be angry with | I need to get out of the house for a bit. My roommate is really angry with me. |
| apply for | We need to apply for the visa ASAP. |
| concentrate on | I need to concentrate on my target practice. |
| consist of | A squad consists of two or three fireteams. |
| die of | The majority of casualties die of blood loss on the field. |
| disagree on | We disagree on most things. |
| escape from | He escaped from the enemy camp. |
| be familiar with | I'm not familiar with this model. |
| insist on | He insists on commanding this mission himself. |
| laugh at | I'm so embarrassed. I feel like the whole squad is laughing at me. |
| be made of | Our uniforms are made of extremely durable material. |

# 2. ANSWER KEY

| be opposed to | He was opposed to the idea. |
|---|---|
| be prepared for | Anything could happen on this mission so you must be prepared for combat. |
| be responsible for | You are responsible for your own gear when you're out on the field. |
| be tired of | I'm sick and tired of the food here! |
| worried about | I'm worried about Smith. He seems really down. |

## LESSON 13 : WAR GAMES

### A Warm Up for Reading

1. Answers will vary.
2. a. in tandem
   b. rehearsal
   c. FTX
   d. warfare
   e. CPX

### B Reading

1. b, c
2. d

3-6. Answers will vary.

### C Grammar : Repeating a Comparative

1. stronger and stronger
2. farther and farther
3. more and more advanced
4. more and more tense

### E Warm Up for Listening

1. assault
2. seize
3. secure
4. combat position
5. passage of lines

### F Listening

1. d
2. d
3. T
4. F – they will go after 1 Platoon
5. T
6. T

### G Grammar : Double Comparatives

1. The swifter the assault, the better our chances of victory.
2. The more powerful the weapons, the more careful we should be.
3. The bigger the mission, the more nervous I get.

## LESSON 14 : MAP READING

### A Warm Up for Reading

1. a. desert
   b. jungle
   c. mountain
   d. arctic
   e. urban

### B Reading

1. a
2. d
3. desert, mountain, jungle, arctic, urban
4. a large scale map
5. concealment
6. 612

### C Grammar : Map Reading

1. river
2. woods
3. hill

### E Warm Up for Listening

a. depression
b. ridge
c. saddle
d. hill
e. valley

### F Listening

1. c
2. b
3. communications center
4. enemy
5. firing position
6. friendly forces

## LESSON 15 : CONVOYS

### A Warm Up for Reading

a. enemy assault
b. medical aid
c. supplies
d. convoy

### B Reading

1. c
2. c
3. driver fatigue / enemy assault / choke points / dangerous intersections
4. maintenance, recovery, medical aid
5. leads the convoy
6. maintenance, supply checks, driver morale

### C Grammar : Non-action Verbs

1. am looking / see
2. is approaching / need
3. believe / possesses

### E Warm Up for Listening

1. choke point
2. release point
3. ETA
4. march column
5. resistance

### F Listening

1. a
2. a, c
3. to move supplies from HQ to the release point while providing protection for the humanitarian aid vehicles
4. 7 hours
5. she thought it would be someone else (Captain Cruise)
6. they will be passing through enemy territory

### G Grammar : Participial Adjectives

1. confusing
2. alarmed
3. exhausted
4. alarming

## LESSON 16 : BRIEFINGS

### A Warm Up for Reading

1. a. T-junction
   b. fork
   c. roundabout
   d. intersection
   e. bridge

### B Reading

1. d
2. c
3. A
4. D
5. G
6. J

Appendix 113

# 2. ANSWER KEY

### C  Grammar : Get + Adjective

1. getting dark
2. getting sleepy
3. gets cold
4. got sick

### E  Warm Up for Listening

1. service station
2. ambush
3. route
4. strip

### F  Listening

1. a
2. a
3. F – the starting point is HQ
4. F – the movement will last 3.5 hours (from 1 p.m. to 4:30 p.m.)
5. F – the first rest area will be 5 kilometers after the roundabout, the rest area is on the B14
6. F – the strip on AF56 is controlled by enemy forces

### G  Grammar : Get + Past Participle

1. get acquainted
2. getting crowded
3. got lost
4. getting killed

# Notes

# Notes

# Notes

# Notes

## Notes

# Notes